Bebo

DAVID CHANDLER IS AN AMERICAN SCHOLAR, MOST WELL-KNOWN as an expert on Cambodia. His sojourn in Phnom Penh as a US foreign service officer in the early 1960s was pivotal in his life. He earned graduate degrees at Yale and Michigan before taking up a position in Monash University's History Department in 1972. His association with Cambodia continued in consultancies with Amnesty International, the UNHCR, the Asia Foundation and several other NGOs. He has published five books on Cambodia and a book of poetry *Marking Time*, which appeared in 2017. After leaving Monash in 1998, he taught for several years at universities in the United States. He returned to Melbourne in 2003, and in retirement, resumed his scholarly work. In 2010 he embarked on a different kind of literary journey, a biography of his mother 'a person I loved, whose company I enjoyed and whom I've been told I resemble in many ways', a woman universally known as 'Bebo'.

Bebo

A Portrait of My Mother

DAVID CHANDLER

K

KERR

Melbourne, Victoria

First printed for private distribution 2021
Kerr Publishing Pty Ltd
Melbourne, Victoria
ABN 64 124 219 638

ISBN 978-1-875703-46-3

Cover photograph: 'Bebo', self portrait oil on canvas 1934

Cover and book design: Paul Taylder of Xigrafix Media and Design

Typeset in Caslon Pro 12/16pt

Print-on-Demand services: Lightning Source

National Library of Australia PrePublication Data Service:

A catalogue record for this
book is available from the
National Library of Australia

In Susan's memory and for Bebo's descendants

Contents

Introduction

AMILY NAMES CAN OFTEN BE CONFUSING. MY MOTHER, christened May Margaret Gabrielle Chanler in 1897, added a "d" to her name when she married my father Porter Chandler in 1924. Hardly anyone who knew her called her "Gabrielle", a name that she used only as a signature. Instead she was known throughout her life by her nickname, Bebo, derived from the Italian word *bebolina* meaning "little pigeon", bestowed on her, it seems, by an Italian nursemaid in Rome when she was very young.

This book is about a person I loved, whose company I enjoyed and whom I've been told I resemble in many ways. I've written it because I was curious to learn more about a life that I felt was intrinsically interesting and partly concealed from view like the lives of many women of Bebo's generation. Once I got started, I found that I had many helpful documents to work with. Finally, making sense of the sources and examining my mother's life in a narrative format appealed to me as a historian.

For several years there was a sense of urgency to the project because I'd put off writing until I was seventy-six years old. Eleven years later, I'm the only one left among Bebo's descendants who can remember what she was like.

When I finished writing, I was eager for my wife, our children and Bebo's younger descendants who never knew her to encounter her in these pages.

Inevitably, perhaps, this book will also tell the story of my parents' thirty-four-year marriage and what they brought to it from their backgrounds, their childhoods and their parents. I need to stress that events in my father's admirable, far more fully documented life crop up often in what follows but the focus for this project has kept me from writing the full-scale biography that he may well deserve.

Once my own memories kick in around 1938 what follows will be a narrative of my life up to Bebo's death twenty years later. My three siblings also have roles to play in the memoir but I will try to keep Bebo on centerstage.

The principal documentary sources that I use are letters that Bebo wrote and received between 1908 and her death. Hundreds of them are housed in the New York Historical Society where my father deposited family papers in 1974. Several of the letters that she wrote to her mother before 1940 are in the Margaret Chanler collection in the Houghton Library at Harvard. My aunt Hester Pickman, Bebo's older sister, presented me with a cache of Bebo's letters in 1977 and more recently I located more than a hundred others among my father's papers.

Many of the letters that people wrote to Bebo have been useful in what follows but I will be privileging the ones that she wrote herself. They have a lively, recognizable voice and a remark-ably consistent point of view. She recognized this consistency in 1956 when she wrote to Hester: "Re-reading my old letters has made me terribly self-conscious. I see myself (when we decide on the final disposal of family letters) saying to myself, 'I haven't changed at all!'"

I regret that the letters she wrote to Porter when he was over-seas in North Africa in 1942–43 were lost when the ship that was carrying — among other things — Porter's footlocker in the summer of 1943 was torpedoed and sank. In his own letters from North Africa, which he collected in 1974, he remarks that Bebo's letters to him "were always enlightening and often pungent." They undoubtedly contained more information about the ebb and flow of her daily life than those she wrote at this time to Hester and her mother. They would certainly have enriched what follows.

Sadly, I saved only one of the letters that she wrote to me between 1947 when I went off to boarding school and 1958 when she died. These were the years of our greatest rapport and her letters were fun to read.

I also realize that the letters I've used, even at their best, can only give snapshots of Bebo, the addresses where she was living and the days when they were written. Snapshots can be misleading sources for making sense of an entire life, for as Kathryn Hughes has perceptively written, "Far from being the full picture of someone's personality, letters provide an angled glance, as distorting as those fun house mirrors that you used to find at the end of piers."[1] This is particularly true in what follows because I base so much of the book on Bebo's letters to only three recipients: her husband, her mother and one of her sisters. Each of them required a different "angled glance."

A second invaluable documentary source for my memoir consists of the medical records that were assembled in 1937 and again in 1953 when Bebo was a patient in what was originally known as the Bloomingdale Hospital in White Plains, NY. She was suffering on both occasions from what used to be called nervous breakdowns. She was a patient at the hospital for nine months in 1937 and for three months in 1953. I visited her in 1953 but her 1937 stay at the hospital, when I was only four, left a blank space in my childhood and in my knowledge of her life. This blank space was for many years a source of intellectual bafflement and concern for me. I simply didn't know what had happened in these hospitalizations, although my mother often said that the treatment she'd received had been humane and helpful.

I requested a copy of Bebo's medical records in 2010, and after they had been reviewed by staff at the Presbyterian Hospital (the successor to Bloomingdale) they were released to me a few months later. They contain many penetrating comments by psychiatrists about Bebo and her afflictions as well as several of her own characteristically frank, perceptive self-assessments. Bebo's was an examined life, analyzed by herself and by several sympathetic, trained observers. Because Bebo was so vulnerable on both occasions the medical records were often saddening to read.

The Bloomingdale records contain some material that I have kept to myself out of respect for Bebo's enduring rights to privacy. At the same time, what I learned from the records in terms of family history sometimes surprised me or amplified what I knew already, taking me between the lines of the narrative that I had already fashioned from my memories, from published sources and from her correspondence.[2]

Finally, while many of my mother's forebears are well documented in a series of readable books, Bebo as a person surfaces here and there in a handful of other printed and oral sources. These include her mother's published memoirs, scattered references in the *New York Times* and the memories of people who knew her and were still alive when I began work on this project.[3]

Although my mother would probably have played down this biographical project (she was one of the least egotistical people I have known) I hope she would have enjoyed meeting her grandchildren and Susan in this way.

Notes

1   Kathryn Hughes, "Famous People are Also Banal", *Guardian Weekly*, February 4, 2011.

2   My friend Peter Judd, an experienced genealogist, showed me how to request the records and Dr Steven Roth, a psychiatrist at the Presbyterian Hospital, reviewed them and permitted their release. I'm grateful for correspondence and telephone conversations with Peter and Dr Roth in 2010–11.

3   Finding the printed references was eased by the extraordinary reach of Google and Google Books. My cousin, the late Nicholas Clifford, and my daughter Maggie helped to retrieve material from the Margaret Chanler papers in the Houghton Library at Harvard.

"Bebolina" Rome c1899

CHAPTER 1

Families in the Background and Bebo's Early Years

MAY MARGARET GABRIELLE CHANLER WAS BORN IN New York City on May 20, 1897. She was the sixth of eight children, seven of whom survived to adulthood.[1] She was the fourth girl. Her parents, Margaret ("Daisy", née Terry, 1862–1952) and Winthrop ("Winty") Chanler (1863–1926), were first cousins once removed, because Daisy's uncle, Samuel Ward (1817–1884) was Winty's maternal grandfather. Bebo spoke often of this close connection. She always felt that it had something to do with the nervousness that she assumed she had inherited but also with the intimacy that knitted her siblings and their descendants together into an affectionate, self-assured and often self-regarding private world.

I begin the story of Bebo's life by describing her parents, the world they lived in and their expectations.

Bebo's mother Margaret Terry Chanler (referred to hereafter as Daisy) was a powerful influence on the lives of her descendants. She was born and brought up in Rome by her American parents Luther Terry (1806–1901), a painter, and Louisa Ward (1823–1897), the widow of the American sculptor Thomas Crawford (1824–1857).

Louisa was the younger sister of Sam Ward and of Julia Ward Howe (1819–1910), the noted poet, abolitionist and advocate of women's rights who wrote "The Battle Hymn of the Republic".[2] Louisa had met Crawford in 1843 in Rome when she was travelling in Europe with the Howes. The couple were married in New York in the following year and returned to Rome where Crawford had a studio. Crawford made a good living as a sculptor and in the 1850s he sculpted the statue of "Liberty" that's on the dome of the US capitol.

There was a sizeable American colony in Rome in the mid to late nineteenth century. Many of them were aspiring artists. As Deborah Clifford has written:

> The Eternal City was very popular with Americans in the 1840s, about a thousand came there every year and they found something in the strangeness of the Latin, Catholic culture that they missed at home.[3]

One of the aspiring artists was Luther Terry, who had left a farm in Enfield, Connecticut, at the age of twenty to travel to Rome, his daughter Daisy later wrote, "on what must have seemed in those days a great adventure."[4] He studied painting in the city and over the years became a moderately successful member of the colony of American artists in Rome. He stayed in the city for the rest of his life without ever becoming fluent in Italian. When his friend Thomas Crawford died in 1857, Luther, who had never married, rallied around the family, paid court to Louisa and after a suitable interval proposed to her. They were married in 1861. Luther was fifty-seven. Louisa was not yet forty.[5]

Daisy Terry was close to her half-brother, the novelist F. Marion Crawford (1854–1909), but unlike him she had little formal schooling and was educated by private tutors. Throughout her life Daisy was an intelligent, aesthetic, inquisitive and ambitious person. She became a skilled horsewoman and a talented pianist and was always an assiduous reader, fluent in four languages. She never adjusted to being American and she maintained a disdainful, often misinformed "European" view of the Western United States.[6] Her two volumes of memoirs, *Roman Spring* (1934) and *Autumn in the Valley* (1936) are elegantly written and were well reviewed. Her last book, *Memory Makes Music* (1949), although less widely circulated, is perceptive and appealing.

At the age of twenty-one Daisy became a Roman Catholic — a momentous decision that took her family by surprise and had a ripple effect on her descendants. She made the leap after a good deal of thought and reading and after a wide-ranging correspondence with her half-brother, who had already become a Catholic.[7] Her rational, considered move upset her Protestant parents and some of her American friends later on. After she married my tolerant, nominally Episcopalian grandfather, her choice of religion distressed two of his anti-Catholic sisters (the third sister, similarly spurned, was an enthusiastic convert to Catholicism). Members of the American East Coast establishment at this time, after all, were overwhelmingly Protestant and their interactions with Catholics were often limited to their contacts with the police and with their Irish servants.

In 1914, when Daisy's daughter Hester was engaged to the Bostonian Edward Pickman, Hester's future mother-in-law wrote to a friend, Mrs Henry Cabot Lodge, who happened also to be a friend of Daisy's: "I understand that Miss Chanler is a Catholic. I had thought we were safe from that sort of thing in Boston." Similarly, when I was at Harvard in the early 1950s, some of my WASP (White Anglo-Saxon Protestant) friends found it inexplicable that I could be a Catholic without being either Irish or Italian.

Daisy described the process and rationale of her conversion

in *Roman Spring*, where she wrote with characteristic self-assurance: "I became a Catholic because I wanted to and I have never for a moment had reason to regret it."[8]

From then on, her religion always played a crucial role in her life. It had a profound, uneven effect on her descendants. Her children were devout Catholics and so were many of her grandchildren, at least for a time. My own commitment, once intense, faded in my thirties but the exigencies and rewards of Catholicism, as we shall see, were part of the texture of Bebo's life and of her husband's and mine for many years.

As she matured, Daisy, like Bebo later on, was always eager to meet and get to know artists, writers, diplomats and musical people whose ideas and achievements appealed to her inquisitive mind. Over the years she made friends with such luminaries as the historian and philosopher Henry Adams,[9] the connoisseur and art historian Bernard Berenson,[10] Senator Henry Cabot Lodge and his wife and the novelists F. Scott Fitzgerald, Henry James and Edith Wharton. She often stayed and travelled with Wharton in Europe in the 1920s and 1930s.[11]

Daisy and Winty's social life and their almost compulsive travels meant that Daisy was often absent and was a seemingly neglectful mother, especially of her younger children, who were cared for by nurses and governesses before they were sent away to school. Once they were grown, however, she sought their company and kept in close touch with them. This attentiveness annoyed the childless Edith Wharton, who wrote impatiently to a cousin in 1931: "I cannot see why [Daisy] cannot let her grown up and thoroughly competent children look after themselves and arrange her life as she pleases."[12]

Many people who knew Bebo's father Winthrop ("Winty") Chanler (1863–1926) remarked on his wit, energy, gallantry and charm. He was born into a wealthy family and along with his seven siblings he inherited a large sum of money when he was orphaned at the age of fourteen. Soon after his parents' deaths Winty spent two years at Eton. In response to my query about his time at the school Ms P. Vickers, the Eton archivist, wrote:

> Your grandfather attended Eton from January 1878 until July 1880, boarding with Mr. Mozley. He did not play in any school teams or win any major school prizes but he was a sufficiently good oarsman to reach the final of Lower Boy Pulling in 1879. No house books survive for that house so I am afraid I have no record of any house activities.[13]

In 1886 Winty graduated from Harvard a year late. He had enjoyed himself as a steeplechase rider, a man about town and as a member of the Porcellian Club.[14] Fellow members of the club, and friends of Winty's, included Theodore Roosevelt and the novelist Owen Wister, as well as a number of New York and Boston socialites who remained his friends for life.[15]

Aside from military service in World War I, Winty never held a paying job. His busy, pleasurable life included innumerable fox hunts in England, Ireland and the United States, many falls from horses, countless hunting expeditions and an adventure running guns into "revolutionary" Cuba in 1898. Winty almost always led exactly the life that he wanted to lead. As one of his sisters once remarked, "Whatever Winty does, his conscience sits looking on beating happy applause."[16]

Intellectually, Daisy and Winty were good companions. Their warm-hearted, witty letters to each other suggest that they shared a wide-ranging interest in the vagaries of social life and a gift for making and keeping friends. They met for the first time in Newport, Rhode Island, in 1882, when Daisy and her family were visiting relatives in the United States and Winty and his siblings were spending the summer in Cliff Lawn, a huge wooden "cottage" built as a summer home for Winty's father John Chanler and his family in 1873.

Daisy recalled in *Roman Spring* that she had found Winty to be "the most entirely charming boy I had ever met." Her rakish, ebullient uncle Sam Ward, Winty's maternal grandfather, introduced them to each other but Daisy's other memories of that summer were less positive:

> I never felt quite in step with the Newport world. I was too foreign; I spoke with a strong Italian accent; I was too much interested in things that in no way pertained to the cogent business of youth ... The fashionable world of Newport seemed dull, wholly taken up with the externals of life ...[17]

Winty and Daisy parted on friendly terms soon afterwards. Winty enrolled at Harvard. In 1885 they met again in Rome and fell in love. Their marriage as cousins of different faiths required several Catholic dispensations, but these were easy for well-connected people to obtain and the wedding took place in Rome in December 1886. Winty and Daisy's marriage lasted for almost forty years and seems to have been a love match on both sides. Daisy told Bebo that friends of Winty's had often remarked to her how unusual it was for a woman of her social position to have a husband who was still in love with her, and faithful.

In 1886 these happy, witty and prosperous participants in a gilded age[18] embarked on a well-heeled life together. They were never concerned about money. Both of them had been raised in comfort. The Wards were a prosperous banking family prominent in "Old New York" with roots in seventeenth-century Rhode Island. Daisy had been brought up in a succession of large apartments carved out of Renaissance and baroque *palazzi*, but the Chanler fortune was more recent and much larger. It sprang from the fact that Winty's maternal grandmother, Emily Astor

(1819–1841) was the granddaughter of John Jacob Astor (1763–1848), a German immigrant who at his death was perhaps the richest man in the United States, with a fortune estimated (in today's dollars) at US$110 billion.

John Jacob's son, William Backhouse Astor (1792–1875), Emily's father, expanded the family fortune by investing in real estate in New York City. Through marriage with a member of the socially prominent Livingston family in the 1830s, William came to own a 43-room house named Rokeby overlooking the Hudson River near Rhinebeck, NY, where Winty and his siblings later grew up. The house and grounds eventually passed to Winty's sister Margaret Aldrich (1870–1963). Several of my second cousins, Margaret's grandchildren, now inhabit different parts of the haunting, somewhat haunted house.[19]

When Emily, who was said to be William Astor's favorite child, was eighteen she married Samuel Ward, then an effervescent, socially acceptable banker, scholar and *bon vivant* who later ran through a series of fortunes, beginning with his own. William Astor gave Rokeby to his daughter as a wedding present.

In the 1860s and 1870s, "Uncle Sam" Ward was one of the first so-called social lobbyists in Washington. He brought legislators and interested outside parties together at dinners that he arranged. He accepted fees for arranging the occasions. These activities took place in the presidency of U.S. Grant that has been condemned by many writers as one of the most corrupt in US history. In the late 1860s "Uncle Sam" negotiated a treaty between the United States and Paraguay and in a long, rich and varied career he befriended the poet Henry Wadsworth Longfellow, the British politician Lord Rosebery and many others.

Sam Ward was a noted gourmand who arranged and hosted sumptuous feasts for US Congressmen and Senators at which issues at stake were only tangentially raised. When he was in funds, he showered his friends and relations with elaborate, well-selected gifts of gems, fine wine and out-of-season fruit. In 1880 the British cartoonist "Spy" immortalized him in the London magazine *Vanity Fair*. His friends and descendants, including Winty and Daisy, recalled him as a large-hearted, buoyant, life-enhancing man. A lethal cocktail named after him consists of chartreuse served with a dash of bitters in a scooped-out lemon rind.[20]

Sam and Emily's marriage was happy but brief. Emily died in 1841 giving birth to their second child, who was stillborn. Their surviving daughter Margaret (1838–1875), known as "Maddie", grew up to be Winty's mother. She was raised almost entirely by the Astors, who broke off relations with Sam Ward because of his "Bohemian" habits and because he remarried "beneath" him relatively soon after Emily's death.[21]

In 1862, when she was 24, Maddie married John Winthrop Chanler (1826–1877), an exuberant, nervous, well-connected New York lawyer and politician who became in the same year a US congressman representing the 7th District (lower Manhattan and parts of Brooklyn) of New York. Chanler's father John White Chanler was an Episcopal clergyman who had come north from South Carolina in his twenties to study divinity at Yale College and had married into New York society, linking his name with the Winthrop and Stuyvesant families.

In Congress, John Chanler was a so-called Peace Democrat, or Copperhead,[22] which meant that he opposed the Civil War, as did many other city-dwellers in the North. He also supported slavery as an institution and in 1865 he voted against the Thirteenth Amendment as well as the two subsequent amendments that granted civil rights to African Americans. In opposing these amendments, he was joined by all of his fellow Democrats in the House of Representatives.

Chanler was re-elected to Congress in 1864 and 1866, on the

Bebo c1909

second occasion after he had been censured by his Congressional colleagues and forced to resign. His bizarre offence was to propose a measure that supported a Presidential veto. Chanler's proposal was considered be an "insult" to the Congress. Some of his Congressional speeches are witty diatribes but others display an ugly strand of racism.[23] He retired from Congress in 1869 when he was only forty-two, allegedly pushed aside by "Boss" Tweed, the corrupt leader of the Democratic Party machine in New York known as Tammany Hall.

In the Bloomingdale papers, Bebo uses the word "irascible" to describe her grandfather. The erratic behavior of some of

Winty's siblings convinced her that the mental unbalance that led to her own hospitalizations in 1937 and 1953 had its roots in her Chanler forebears rather than among the Wards and Terrys.

Maddie bore John Chanler ten children. Eight of them survived to adulthood. She died in 1875 after catching a chill at her grandfather Astor's funeral. John Chanler died two years later from what some contemporaries said was a broken heart. Their surviving children were gleefully dubbed the "Astor Orphans" by the New York press. They grew up at Rokeby where they were chaperoned by a spinster cousin from South Carolina, occasional tutors and a congenial staff of servants.

It's important to remember that the orphans weren't technically Astors. They were the children of an Astor granddaughter who had been remembered handsomely in her father's will. In other words, the orphans (and their descendants, like me) had no further access to the gigantic, ever-expanding Astor fortune.

Bebo Chanler, then, was born into a close-knit, wealthy, cultivated family. Some of its entanglements seemed excessive to her later on and Bebo and her siblings were shadowed to an extent by the often-flamboyant behavior of the "Astor orphans," especially the males, who enjoyed anarchic, relatively unschooled childhoods. When they grew up, all the brothers drank and talked too much. They entertained grandiose views of themselves and enjoyed the limelight. One of them escaped from an insane asylum, another was married briefly to an opera singer who took most of his money and a third named a waterfall in East Africa after himself during a self-financed exploration of the region. Winty shared the restlessness and conviviality of his brothers but unlike most of them he was happily married, more focused and less anarchic.[24]

Bebo was also born into the gilded, cosmopolitan and intellectually shallow world of the turn-of-the century American north-east, described in the novels of Daisy's friend Edith

Wharton and later in those of Louis Auchincloss (1917–2010), whose mother Priscilla, ten years Bebo's senior, was probably Bebo's closest friend.[25]

An eccentric herself, Bebo tolerated and enjoyed eccentricity in others but she took no pride in her uncles and never traded on her inherited social position. At the same time, her privileged background gave her a devil-may-care self-confidence and a life-long aversion to comparing herself to others. She had little interest in seeking attention and no urge to move up some kind of social ladder. She was class conscious but never paid homage to anyone or demeaned anyone because of their social status. Two of her nieces told me that she was the "freest spirit" either of them had known and her friend Louis Auchincloss concurred, writing me that:

> I think she was one of the most truly independent souls I ever knew. Of course, her social and intellectual background was such that no outward manifestations of wealth or power could impress her. Was anyone better born, or brighter, or more international or even more "into" sports than the Chanlers? But Bebo's independence did not depend on that. It depended on the bedrock of her sane sense of values. She was devoid of personal vanity; perhaps she should have done a little more about her clothes and appearance. But the eagerness in her thrusting head when a subject grabbed her interest, the way she seemed to take it in her teeth and tear at it was wonderful, and her tense Chanler laugh when something was ridiculous seemed to dispose of it forever.[26]

To an extent, Bebo inherited her character from her parents. Her free-spiritedness and her sense of humour, I'd suggest, came from her father and she inherited her high intellectual and aesthetic standards as well as her religious faith from Daisy. In

Chanler family at Cliff Lawn, Newport, Rhode Island
1902: Bebo aged 5, far right

some ways she broke from them both but she was never disloyal to them or indifferent to what they had given her. Like Daisy and Winty, Bebo was easily bored and people who failed to interest her could find her abrupt and difficult to deal with.

Once she grew up her genuine interest in people of different backgrounds from her own was in some sense a rejection of the Philistine society into which she had been born and also an extension of Daisy's wide-ranging search for interesting people. Unlike her parents, Bebo was not a name-dropper or a social snob and she seldom put her own "amusement" (a favorite word of Daisy's) ahead of her spiritual life and the welfare of her family even though her husband and her four children (to say nothing of her God) placed demands on her that she was often psychologically unable to meet.

After several years spent living in Washington, DC, New

York City and the gated community of Tuxedo Park, NY, Winty and Daisy moved to Rome in 1897, where Daisy's mother had recently died. They wanted be with Daisy's aged father, who had stayed on in Rome and was to die in 1900.

Bebo earned her life-long nickname during these early years and her first language was Italian. While she was in Rome she almost died from double pneumonia and diphtheria. Later on, she caught scarlet fever and by 1908 when she was eleven, she gleefully told Porter Chandler, the nine-year old boy she later married, that while he had many more toys (as indeed he did, as a cosseted only child) she had had more diseases.

In early 1898, caught up in the endemic anti-Spanish mood in the United States, Winty left Rome to join a Cuban insurrectionist unit that invaded Cuba from Florida in June, aiming to oust the Spanish colonial regime.[27] In the course of this excursion a Spanish bullet hit Winty in the elbow but he escaped successfully and later referred to these adventures as "the happiest time of his life." Unlike his brother William, who was a Rough Rider with their mutual friend Teddy Roosevelt alongside my father's cousin Craig Wadsworth, Winty didn't take part in the Spanish American War.[28] On January 18, 1899, however, Theodore Roosevelt, then governor of New York, wrote him that "I have always regretted that you were not with our regiment but you did first rate work and you got an honorable wound; after all, what more could you wish?"[29]

Soon after Luther Terry's death in 1900 the family returned to America and settled for a time in Newport, Rhode Island, in the sumptuous "cottage" called Cliff Lawn that Winty had inherited in his father's will. Winty sold Cliff Lawn in 1904. It is now The Chanler, an expensive boutique hotel.

Bebo's youngest brother Theodore (1902–1961), always known as Teddy, was born in Newport. Later famous as a composer, he was named after his godfather, President Theodore Roosevelt,

Bebo in feathered hat c1908

who travelled to Newport for the christening. Teddy's godmother was Mrs Henry Cabot Lodge, the wife of the Massachusetts senator whom Winty and Daisy had befriended in Washington in the 1880s. Edith Wharton, a childhood friend of Daisy's, was among the two dozen invited guests.[30]

There is little documentation for the next few years of Bebo's life, although a photograph of her aged seven or eight, wearing a grown-up's feathered hat, inspired a poem that I wrote a century later:

> She's borrowed someone's hat
> or someone's tied it on—
> its brim and ostrich feathers
> construct an aureole around her face
> blending a belle époque sirène
> with someone small and vulnerable:
> she's eight. Oh dear.
> Across a hundred years
> she almost manages to smile.

In 1906 Winty purchased Sweetbriar Farm, which consisted of a spacious, recently built house and 160 acres of pasture outside the village of Geneseo in the prosperous rolling landscape of western New York state. He and Daisy were drawn to the area by its excellent fox-hunting, a sport at which they both excelled.[31] The Chanlers also welcomed a comfortable house that could shelter their large family and the staff they felt they needed. Although they travelled constantly, Winty and Daisy made Sweetbriar their "home" until Winty died in 1926 and it was Daisy's home as a widow until she moved to Boston in 1940. Bebo's brother Hubert (1900–1974) inherited the house from his mother in 1952 and it remained in the family until 1979.

In the years between buying Sweetbriar and the outbreak of World War I, the Chanlers wintered in New York City, Washington, London or Paris, returning to Geneseo for the summer and for fox-hunting in the fall.[32] Their children were farmed out to boarding schools by the time they were ten years old and joined their parents in Geneseo for their summer vacations. Bebo often spoke fondly of the complex family theatricals at Sweetbriar that had been scripted by her sister Hester and acted out by her siblings and local children in the rough and tumble of what became, whenever it assembled, a happy, talented and energetic family. Bebo remained especially close to Teddy and Hester for the rest of her life.[33]

Notes

1   Bebo's eldest brother John Winthrop Chanler II died in a sledding accident in Tuxedo Park, NY when he was six. See Appendix A below.

2   Louise Hall Tharp, *Three Saints and a Sinner*. Boston, 1959 is a pleasing composite biography of the Ward siblings. See also Deborah Pickman Clifford, *Mine Eyes Have Seen the Glory*. Boston, 1978, a spirited biography of Julia Ward Howe. Deborah, my first cousin, always maintained that our Ward forebears were more gifted and interesting than the Chanlers even though (and perhaps partly because) they attracted less attention in the press. On Julia see also Elaine Showalter, The *Civil Wars of Julia Ward Howe*. New York, 2016.

3   Clifford, *Mine Eyes Have Seen the Glory*, p. 75. See also Paul Baker, *The Fortunate Pilgrims: Americans in Rome, 1800–1860*. New York, 1965.

4   Mrs Winthrop Chanler, *Roman Spring*. Boston, 1934, pp. 3–4. For more on Luther Terry, see Tharp, *Three Saints*, pp. 271–74.

5   The couple had two children—Daisy and her younger brother Arthur. In September 2014 I came across a letter from Luther to Daisy, dated 1889. This was the only occasion in my years of research that I'd overheard his voice. The cozy and intimate six-page letter suggested that his relationship with his daughter was close.

6   In 1900, Daisy's husband Winty wrote his friend Owen Wister that Daisy was "hampered by a foreign bringing up and a total dislike of the [American] West". Owen Wister, *Roosevelt: The Story of a Friendship*. New York, 1934, p. 169. Daisy's first experience of the region occurred in 1879 when she stayed at a cousin's California ranch. She wrote later, "my Rome-sick spirit found it hard to live on mere landscape, and life at the ranch seemed stripped of all interest." Chanler, *Roman Spring*, p. 107. A second exposure to California in 1939, visiting her son Hubert (she read Doughty's *Arabia Deserta* on the transcontinental rail journey), was a self-inflicted disaster. She never went West again.

7   I have inherited some of the free-ranging letters that Crawford wrote to Daisy at this time. The heroine of his novel *Katherine Lauderdale* (1894) is based on Daisy but by then the two had become estranged, because Crawford disliked Winty Chanler and his gilded social circle. See Jane Hanna Pease, *Romantic Novels, Romantic Novelist: Francis Marion Crawford*. Bloomington, IN, 2011, pp. 83–84.

8   Chanler, *Roman Spring*, p. 148. She discusses her conversion on pp. 128–46. Fur an earlier account of her experiences, see also Georgina Pell Curtis (ed.), *Some Roads to Rome: Being Personal Records of Conversion to the Catholic Church*. St Louis, MO 1910), pp. 83–84, a passage supplied by Daisy to Ms Curtis. I'm grateful to my cousin Daisy Welch for providing this reference.

9   Henry Adams (1838–1918), the grandson and great grandson of US presidents, was an astute observer of US history and the US political scene. In the closing years of his life, he was probably the closest thing that America had to a national intellectual. His most famous books are *Mont St Michel and Chartres* (1904) and *The Education of Henry Adams* (1907). He befriended Winty and Daisy in the early 1900s and was an honorary "uncle" to their children, including Bebo.

10   Bernard Berenson (1865–1959) was a pre-eminent art historian specializing in Italian Renaissance art. After emigrating to America from Russia in 1875, he attended Harvard and by the early 1900s he had published several path-breaking books. He settled in a villa named I Tatti outside Florence and bequeathed it to Harvard when he died. For his eulogy for Daisy, see Appendix B below.

11   On Daisy's friendship with Edith Wharton (1862–1937), see Hermione Lee, *Edith Wharton*. London, 2005, *passim*. Unfortunately, the portrait of "Margaret Chanler", supposedly of Daisy in Lee's biography, is of Daisy's hostile sister-in-law, Margaret Chanler, who had that name before she married Richard Aldrich. See also Louis Auchincloss, "Edith Wharton and Margaret Chanler", in his *Love Without Wings: Friendships in Literature and Politics*. New York, 1991, pp. 47–58; and Janet Flanner, "Dearest Edith", *New Yorker*, 22 February 1929. On Daisy's friendship with Fitzgerald, see Andrea Olmstead, *Who Was F. Scott Fitzgerald's Daisy?* Smashwords.com, 2012.

12   Quoted in Lee, *Edith Wharton*, p. 680. Daisy once remarked that if the devil were ever to appear to teenagers, Wharton would take the form of a small child. Bebo's bêtes noires, I think, would have taken the form of teenagers.

13   P. Vickers, email, November 22, 2010.

14   Winty was elected President of the Porcellian in his senior year.

15   Amos Tuck French (ed.), *Some Letters from Chan 1886–1926: To a Chosen Few*. Chester, NH, 1939, collects letters from Winty, written largely to French (1863–1941), a college classmate and in later life a New York banker. Winty, Roosevelt and Wister were also members of the Boone and Crockett Club, a convivial society founded by Roosevelt in 1886 dedicated to big game hunting. In a book about the sport edited by Roosevelt in the 1890s, Winty contributed a chapter on hunting elk in Wyoming.

16   Wister, *Roosevelt: The Story of a Friendship*, p. 180. Pages 176–84 of this memoir are about Winty Chanler, who also crops up elsewhere in the book.

17   Chanler, *Roman Spring*, p. 121.

18   The phrase, contrasted with a more genuine golden age, originated with Mark Twain, whose novel written with Samuel Warner, *A Gilded Age: A Tale of Today*, was published in 1873 — the heyday of Sam Ward's work as a lobbyist.

19   The architect Stanford White (1853–1906) modernized Rokeby in the 1890s. Bebo's sister Laura (1887–1984) married White's son Lawrence Grant White ("Larry", 1887–1955) in 1916. On Rokeby nowadays, see Richard Severo, "Where Heathcliff is Just the Boy Next Door", *New York Times*, June 10, 1975; and Penelope Connor, "In a Crumbling House, Creativity and History Meet", *New York Times*, July 22, 2010. My cousin Richard Aldrich took Susan and me through the house with another second cousin, my college classmate Ben La Farge, in May 2010. Richard's daughter has written a poignant memoir about her unhappy childhood in the benighted house. See Alexandra Aldrich, *The Astor Orphan*. New York, 2013.

20   See Chanler, *Roman Spring*, pp. 152–58; and Maud Howe Elliott, *Sam Ward and his Circle*. Boston, 1938. Ms Elliot, a daughter of Julia Ward Howe, was therefore, like Daisy, Sam Ward's niece. See also Lately Thomas, *Sam Ward King of the Lobby*. Boston, 1965, while Kathryn Alamong Jacob, *King of the Lobby: The Life and Times of Sam Ward*. Baltimore, 2010, repeats many of Thomas's anecdotes word for word without acknowledgement. Sam's nephew F. Marion Crawford (Daisy's half-brother) immortalized him in Dr *Claudius*, an admiring, well-received novel.

21   For details of the estrangement see Thomas, *Sam Ward*, pp. 133-35 and Elliot, *Uncle Sam Ward and his Circle*, pp. 390 ff.

22   On the censure, see *The Congressional Globe*, May 14, 1866, pp. 2573-2575. The vote was 73-20, with 81 abstentions, On the Copperheads, see Jennifer Weber, *Copperheads: The Rise and Fall of Lincoln's Enemies in the North*. New York, 2004. Chanler's name does not appear in this absorbing study. The *New York Times* December 21, 1860 printed the text of a "Manifesto" by a committee of New York City Democrats including Chanler that bemoaned the election of Lincoln, feared war and stated that the "negro race" *[sic]* was well treated under slavery.

23   See for example Iven Bernstein, *The New York City Draft Riots*. New York, 1990, p. 146, quoting one of Chanler's speeches: "Shall the white laborer bow his independent, honored brow to the level of the Negro just set free from slavery, and by …the entrance of the great citadel of the nation, surrender the mastery of his race"? See also *Congressional Globe*, 39th Congress (1865), p. 47, where Chanler says, "I hope that the purity of the white man, the representation of the white race and the sovereignty of these people will be maintained boldly in the face of prejudice". See also David Quigley, *Second Founding: New York City, Reconstruction and the Making of American Democracy*. New York 2005, pp. 47–52, a compendium of Chanler's overheated racist remarks.

24   For a vivid composite history of the Chanlers, see Lately Thomas, *A Pride of Lions*. New York, 1971 and an expanded version, *The Astor Orphans*. Albany, 1999.

25 For an overview of the Gilded Age see Eric Homberger, *Mrs Astor's New York*. New Haven, 2002. Priscilla's husband Howland was a partner of the New York law firm of Davis Polk where my father worked from 1929 until shortly before his death in 1979. Larissa MacFarquhar, "East Side Story" *The New Yorker* February 25, 2008, is a pleasing profile of Louis Auchincloss. When writing elsewhere about his mother, Auchincloss called Bebo the "friend who knew her best."

26 Louis Auchincloss, letter of August 8, 2000.

27 See *New York Times*, June 24, 1898. The 200-man unit included twelve Americans, several of them Porcellians, under Winty's command. See Evan Thomas, *The War Lovers: Roosevelt, Lodge, Hearst and the Rise of Empire*. New York, 2010, especially pp 242–44, 352 and 358.

28 See Thomas, *Pride of Lions*, pp. 254ff; and Chanler, *Autumn in the Valley*, p. 167.

29 Elting R. Morison (ed.), *The Letters of Theodore Roosevelt* Vol. 2. Cambridge, MA, 1951, p. 910.

30 See Lee, *Edith Wharton*, p. 155; and R.W.B. Lewis, *Edith Wharton: A Biography*. New York, 1975, p. 112. It occurs to me that the ceremony, with these godparents, could not have been a Catholic one. I'm not sure what (or if) Catholic arrangements were made beforehand or afterwards. Teddy in any case was a life-long Catholic.

31 W. Austin Wadsworth (1847–1918), a fellow Porcellian, founded the Genesee Valley Hunt in 1876. The sport had occasionally drawn Winty to Geneseo in the 1890s. See Chanler, *Autumn in the Valley*, pp. 43–4.

32 Ellis Island records, for example, reveal that Daisy and her six oldest children travelled together to Europe on January 20, 1906 and returned on May 27.

33 Chanler, *Autumn in the Valley*, pp. 65ff.

Pencil drawing of Bebo by Laura Chanler c1907

CHAPTER 2

Chandlers and Wadsworths

TURNING TO MY FATHER'S FAMILY BACKGROUND, IT'S important to stress that the year he was born, 1899, was an *annus horribilis* from which his mother and her mother never fully recovered. In that year my paternal grandfather, also named Porter (1869–1899), died of a ruptured appendix after less than three years of marriage, five months before his only child, named after him, was born. At that point his widow, Mary Wadsworth Chandler (1866–1927), who never remarried, was thirty-three.

Soon after my father was born, his maternal grandfather Charles Wadsworth (1835–1899) died of cancer. Charles' widow Jessie Burden Wadsworth (1840–1917) lived on in the large Greek revival house three miles west of Geneseo that Charles had purchased in 1872. The five-bedroom house came with several acres of lawns, two gardens, barns and stables and fifty acres of pasture as well as two thousand acres of adjoining farmland. The capacious downstairs rooms had fourteen-foot ceilings. The house wasn't named "Westerly" until 1928, but I'll use that name from now on to distinguish it from Sweetbriar, four miles or so to the east. Both houses will be powerful presences in what follows.

Jessie Wadsworth's thirty-five-year marriage started well but it was never as happy as Mary's far briefer one. The deaths of Charles and Porter in 1899 left these two powerful women lonely and bereft. By that time, they were probably also estranged from one another.

Mary was her parents' only child. She grew up in Westerly and was educated by private tutors. When Jessie died, she inherited the house and the farmland that went with it. When my parents married in 1924, Mary handed over the estate to her son and moved into the village of Geneseo. Westerly and the adjoining land stayed in the family until Porter's death in 1979.

I spent every summer at Westerly until I was seventeen and parts of many summers after that until the late 1960s. For me, the house and the times I spent in it are important ingredients of what Henry James, referring in part to childhood, called a "writer's capital."

Porter's father was the second son and youngest child of a career Navy officer, Ralph Chandler (1829–1889), who died in Hong Kong as a rear admiral in command of the US Asiatic Station.[1] Ralph had been born and raised in Batavia, NY, some twenty miles west of Geneseo. In 1845 he enrolled in the first graduating class of the US Naval Academy. He had a long and distinguished career, spent almost entirely at sea, including a sojourn in Australia and New Zealand in 1874. In 1886, his son Porter was admitted to the Academy. He lasted barely a semester before being expelled for academic reasons.[2]

The factors that led to his poor performance are impossible to determine. He may have felt that his father had forced him into the academy and he seems to have been severely "hazed" but his grades and conduct were unsatisfactory from the start. More to the point, perhaps, Porter seems to have been physically unready for military life. He was seventeen, six feet tall and weighed less than 120 pounds.

Moreover, the year 1886 was an unsettling one for him. His brief academy career overlapped with the departure of his parents and his two unmarried sisters for Japan and also with a crisis in the life of his erratic older brother Redfield (1860–1922), who had run into trouble at his grace and favor post at the New York Navy Yard where Ralph had been commanding officer in 1884–86. After having been fired and reinstated at the yard in October 1886 Redfield allegedly "spent a week in a Chinese den" in New York City and by the end of December was "lost to the sight of his friends."[3]

After young Porter was dismissed from Annapolis, he spent some time with his married sister Bessie Parker in Batavia before going off to work as a cowboy in Texas and Wyoming. There was a rumor in the family that he was partly the model for the hero of Owen Wister's novel *The Virginian* but I have no corroboration of this. The rumor gains plausibility from the fact that Wister, a good friend of Winty's, often stayed at Sweetbriar and Porter's name may have come up in conversation.

Porter's nephew Ralph Chandler Parker (1884–1979) remembered him fondly, and told us in family gatherings that in the late 1890s, after he came back East, Porter could perform rope tricks he had learned as a cowboy and had also remembered from his Annapolis days the commands needed to move a warship in full sail out of port. Ralph Parker was a charming, very tall man who looked a lot like my father, his first cousin. He spent forty-five years in the US Navy, retiring as a captain.

At some point in 1896 Porter returned to Batavia[4] to resume contact with his family. He also needed surgery to remove two bullets from his leg. On June 1, he attended his sister Cornelia's wedding in Batavia. His nephew Ralph Parker, then aged twelve, remembered Porter as "tall, lean, brown and handsome." At the wedding Porter met Mary Wadsworth, then thirty, who was a close friend of his sisters Cornelia and Bessie. After a whirl-wind courtship Porter and Mary were married in Geneseo three months later. According to Ralph Parker, in a letter to my father, when Porter asked Charles Wadsworth for his blessing on the engagement, he said, "Even the clothes on my back are borrowed, but I think I can make your daughter happy." Shortly before the wedding, Bessie wrote to Mary about her brother:

> I have stood by him in his darkest days. He inherits many ways, and my father was the noblest man I ever knew. He was honest and manly and true … [Porter] comes to you empty-handed.

The phrase "empty-handed" suggests with justice that my grandfather brought no money to a marriage that seems like Daisy and Winty's to have been a love match for them both. Porter was almost literally a knight (or cowpoke) on a white horse who swept Mary away from her troubled, almost dysfunctional family all too briefly into a brighter, far more pleasing life.

The couple travelled to Japan for their honeymoon to visit one of Porter's sisters who had had married a British businessman in Yokohama. In late November, they attended a chrysanthe-mum-viewing ceremony in Tokyo given by the Empress.[5] They eventually returned to Geneseo with some unwieldy ceramics and a dozen playful *netsuke*.[6] At that point, Porter's father-in-law asked him to manage his estate and Porter became an active member of the Genesee Valley Hunt. In January 1899 Porter's stomach pains were misdiagnosed by a local doctor and he died of a ruptured appendix. I can't help speculating about what my father's life—or my grandmother's, or mine—would have been like had he lived into the 1900s.

Mary received many letters of condolence after her husband died. A touching one came from Porter's nephew, thirteen-year-old Ralph Parker, who wrote her that "I will always try to be like uncle Porter—as brave, as kind, and as unselfish." Ralph Parker, who died in his nineties, was one of the most honorable people I ever met.

Mary Wadsworth Chandler, for her part, was a strong, beneficial influence on her son and so, by and large, was his somewhat daunting Wadsworth heritage. Mary's father Charles Wadsworth was a wealthy, talented man whose cosseted childhood and youth seem to have spoilt him. He had a poor business sense and a serious drinking problem in later life but the seemingly exotic years that he spent in Paris before he married and the fact that he was a black sheep of our law-abiding family appealed to me when I was growing up. His extensive, leather bound library at Westerly—including several hundred French books that I inherited—is suggestive of a person with serious intellectual interests.[7]

Charles was born into a prosperous, locally prominent family. He was the eldest son of James Wadsworth (1809–1864), whose father, also James (1766–1845), had come from Connecticut to settle in the Genesee valley with his brother William in 1790, "purchasing" vast tracts of land from unwary Native Americans. Charles' father owned tens of thousands of acres in western New York and Ohio as well as a house in New York City.[8] His wife was a Wharton of Philadelphia and the Wadsworth mansion in Geneseo was modelled after the residence of Lord Hertford in Regent Street in London. To honor this fact alongside the Wadsworths' Connecticut ancestry, the house, built in 1835, became known as Hartford House.[9]

Western New York prospered in the heyday of the Erie Canal, which was opened in 1825 and transported wheat and dairy products to New York City until railroads replaced it in the 1850s. The prosperity brought by the canal is reflected in the handsome Greek revival houses dating from the 1830s and 1840s that

Students at Roehampton c1911. Bebo middle row wearing a medal

dot the landscape and line the streets of villages throughout the region, including Geneseo. Westerly, built in 1850 from an 1830 "Florentine" design, is an elegant example of the style.

After being dismissed from Harvard for rowdiness and his failure to attend church services, James Wadsworth studied law for a while and then became, perhaps surprisingly, a conscientious farmer and a generous landlord. He was a founding member of the Republican Party, a benefactor of many local causes and active in the anti-slavery movement. He was the Republican candidate for governor of New York in 1862 but was defeated by the Submissionist-Democrat Henry Seymour, after he had courageously given an abolitionist speech that was unpopular in New York City. Interestingly, the election that Wadsworth lost brought John Chanler to Washington as a Submissionist-Democrat Member of Congress.

When the Civil War began in 1861 Wadsworth had raised a regiment for service in Livingston County known popularly as the "Wadsworth Guards" and at fifty-two he enlisted in the army himself. He had no military experience but was a natural leader. He rose to the rank of brevet major general, led a division at Gettysburg and was popular with his troops. A Confederate sniper fatally wounded him as he led a charge in the Battle of the Wilderness in May 1864. Wadsworth was one of only four Union army generals to be killed in action in the Civil War.[10]

Charles must have found his father a difficult act to follow but for a time his career was impressive in its own way. After a year at Harvard, he enrolled in 1854 in the prestigious École des Mines in Paris, graduating as a mining engineer with honors five years later. His time in Paris overlapped with the early years of the Second Empire, the publication of Flaubert's *Madame Bovary* and Baudelaire's *Les fleurs du mal*. It also coincided with the beginnings of Baron Haussman's dramatic remodelling of the city.[11]

Charles' fastidious notebooks at the École and his well-received thesis have survived and so have many wheedling letters written from Paris, where he incurred substantial debts that he failed to explain.[12] On an allowance of $5000 a year, comparable to at least $100,000 today, he often complained to her that he was unable to make ends meet. In one letter he pleaded for money to purchase a velvet smoking jacket. Years later when I fell in love with Paris, I was pleased by this raffish family connection to the city but Charles' largely importunate letters never describe the non-academic life that I assume (and hope) he was leading.

In 1861 soon after he had returned to America Charles

established an iron works in Buffalo, NY, in partnership with a man named Palmer. The iron works soon fell into debt, an event that drew a severe letter from his father.

In the following year, perhaps to compensate for this misadventure, Charles followed his father's lead and joined the Union army as a lieutenant attached to a regiment being raised in Buffalo. In February 1863, his father tried to obtain his services as an aide-de-camp, but his request was denied,[13] and as a captain Charles saw battle later in the year at Port Hudson, Louisiana, where a fifth of his company was killed. Charles was promoted to the rank of acting major for his bravery in this encounter.[14]

In those days it was permissible to resign a commission in the middle of a war, as Charles did in 1864, shortly before his father's death, in order to return to his business in Buffalo. In September of that year, he married Jessie, the youngest daughter of Henry Burden (1791–1871), an immigrant from Scotland whose iron works in Troy, NY, had supplied most of the horseshoes used by the Union army.[15] An affectionate, welcoming letter from General Wadsworth to Charles' fiancée has survived, written a month before the general was killed. At the same time, he wrote Charles presciently, "I cannot get rid of some anxiety about your great establishment in Buffalo—no dividends and constantly increasing debt."[16]

Using some of the funds inherited from his father, Charles established the Wadsworth Iron Works in Buffalo in 1865. For the next five years the business prospered and the Wadsworths were active in Buffalo society. Their daughter Mary was born in 1866. Charles was a fond and doting father, as his letters to his mother at this time attest. In 1871, however, the iron works failed but the family's finances were cushioned by the fact that James Burden died in the same year and provided generously for his twelve children.

Charles was declared bankrupt in 1872, and court cases to recover his substantial embezzlements from his father's will continued until his death. In 1872 Charles returned to the Genesee valley, where he purchased Westerly and some 2000 acres of nearby farmland.[17] By then, his younger brother James had moved into Hartford House (faintly visible from Westerly's east-facing front porch) and had taken over the management of what had been the general's land. Charles' mother died in 1872, the *annus horribilis* in which Charles was declared bankrupt and moved back to Geneseo. She left Hartford House to James, a decision undoubtedly made some time before her death that may have hurt Charles and certainly offended his brother Craig, who seems to have been traumatized by his experiences in the Civil War and died soon after his mother.[18] Quixotically, Charles joined the Democratic Party at this time, perhaps resenting his brother's enhanced status and perhaps also posthumously defying his father.[19]

At the Centennial Exhibition in Philadelphia in 1876 Charles' short-horn cattle, a breed that he had helped to introduce from England into the United States, won prizes, but soon afterwards his behavior became erratic, affected by continuing rifts with his brother James and his sisters induced by his siphoning of funds from their father's estate. His binge drinking seems to have begun in earnest at this time. When he was drinking seriously, he sometimes used the library on the ground floor as a bedroom where he could be locked in, guarded by the family's coachman. On some occasions, according to Bebo's medical records, he threatened to kill his wife.[20]

Jessie Wadsworth was a pious Presbyterian with settled views and a strong, self-confident personality. She was devoted to her church and also to the house, the estate and more generally to good works, serving on several statewide charitable boards.

Her husband's business failures and excessive drinking must have distressed her and so did the large amounts of money—at least $200,000, worth millions today—that he diverted over the years from his father's estate. Nonetheless, the couple remained together and Charles continued to be intermittently active in politics and local affairs. In 1890, for example, he served as chairman of the committee organising the celebrations of Geneseo's hundredth birthday.

Bebo's medical records from 1937 suggest that Jessie and her daughter Mary were estranged from each other because Mary as a "little girl" in family quarrels had taken the side of her father after being told by her mother, "Choose between me and your father; I can't stand it."

Before 2010 when I was given access to these records I had never heard of the estrangement, which probably explains why Mary didn't move in with her mother after they were both widowed in 1899. In a grim, informal epitaph for Jessie, Mary told my mother who related the line to a psychiatrist in 1937 that "A mother can only be a shining example or a horrid warning."

Jessie's married life and much of Mary's childhood must have been prolonged ordeals. Once the family settled in Westerly and Charles had become a problem drinker, a good deal of Jessie's time was spent in keeping up appearances and running the day-to-day business of heir large, isolated estate. Compensations came from her religion and her work with worthy causes. Her solitary trip every Sunday to and from the Presbyterian Church in Geneseo—to say nothing of their meals with Charles and Mary—can only have intensified her humiliation and unhappiness,[21] but marriages among people of her class in nineteenth-century America were virtually impossible to escape, at least on the grounds that the participants were incompatible or unhappy.

My father grew up as an only child alongside two widowed, lonely, strong-minded women, without many playmates but with a fond and competent Canadian governess, Alice Farncomb, who remained his friend for life. Porter visited her in Canada from time to time, and they exchanged frequent letters. A small oil portrait of her as a young woman hung in the library at Westerly. I see now that she must have acted as a buffer between Porter and the uneasy relationship that persisted between his mother and grandmother. Before he went off to boarding school in Massachusetts in 1909, Porter had no male role models to follow. Instead, the ghosts of his short-lived, charming father and of his once promising, embarrassing grandfather probably haunted his childhood but unlike Bebo he seldom spoke about these years and what may seem to us to have been obvious traumas apparently had no lasting psychological effects.

However, because Porter never talked about what this period was "really like" (the topic was apparently as taboo for him as sexuality), there's no sure way of telling. We do know that he was deeply devoted to his mother, a daunting dowager with a robust sense of humor who was just as devoted to him but who also worked hard to allow him room to breathe. Porter travelled to Europe with his mother in 1906, 1910 and 1914 and they travelled to North Africa and Italy together in 1922. Once Porter was married, Mary and Bebo established a good rapport although Bebo wrote Hester in 1926 that she didn't plan to spend more than a week on holiday in Westerly that summer "because Poggy [Mary's nickname] wears us both out."

With hindsight it's clear that Porter's sunny, bookish temperament adjusted to the hand he had been dealt and triumphed over what appear to me and appeared to Bebo to have been adverse psychological conditions. His drive to succeed academically and in his legal career may have been intended consciously or not to make up for Charles' shortcomings but he never explained his life in this way. His rare comments about Jessie, who died when he was eighteen, depicted her as affectionate, distant and severe.

In any case whenever he dined at Westerly Porter sat at the head of Charles and Jessie's table in the only armchair, an indication he was quick to absorb that he was a Wadsworth as well as a Chandler, the heir to Westerly and the land that went with it. No one else sat in the chair when Porter was somewhere else. In her medical records, Bebo said that this privileged seating arrangement, which grated on her, began when Porter was three years old.

In a comical footnote, when Susan and I spent the summer of 1968 at Westerly and when Porter was working in New York City, Susan sat inadvertently in the armchair on one occasion at lunch. Later that afternoon a chunk of the ceiling above the chair fell harmlessly into the room.

Porter probably always expected to spend part of every year for the rest of his life in this large, inherited house while Bebo, starting as a teenager, longed to escape for good from Sweetbriar and Geneseo. She often told me that had the choice been hers to make she would have preferred to have a summer house in Connecticut within striking distance of New York City. Needless to say, she was never given such a choice.

Notes

1   See Ralph Chandler's obituary in the *New York Times*, February 27, 1889;
    and Porter Chandler, "How My Grandfather Almost Lost the Civil War",
    American Neptune 33 (January 1973), pp. 5–15, drawing on Ralph Chandler's
    manuscript journal now in the New York Historical Society.

2   Professor Richard Ruth, who teaches history at the Naval Academy, generously
    accessed the woeful records of my grandfather's sojourn there.

3   *New York Times*, December 1, 12 and 28, 1886. Redfield didn't attend his
    brother's wedding ten years later. My father never met his uncle and was
    curious about him. Using pre-internet methods, he tracked Redfield to New
    Orleans, where he married in a Catholic ceremony, aged 37, in 1901. He died
    there in 1922, leaving a widow and three children named Ralph, Leroy and
    Gladys, who were all living in Los Angeles in 1941.

4   Ralph Chandler's father, Daniel Hicks Chandler (1795–1864), a lawyer, left
    Upper Granville, NY, on the Vermont border (his forebears had lived in
    Massachusetts) in the 1820s and helped to found the village of Batavia, NY.
    He is buried there although in the 1840s he moved to Wisconsin and became
    a judge in Milwaukee, where he died. I'm grateful to Professor Kathleen
    Kutolowski of SUNY Brockport for information about him and the early years
    of Batavia. See her book *The Social Composition of Political Leadership: Genesee
    County New York, 1811–1860*. New York, 1989.

5   My Monash colleague Adam Clulow has kindly translated the invitation to
    the ceremony, which reads: "Her Majesty the Empress has instructed the
    minister of the Imperial Household to respectfully invite Porter Chandler
    (Poruta Chandoru) and his wife to participate in chrysanthemum viewing on
    the 21st day (of November) 1896 in the afternoon at 2:30 pm at the gardens of
    the Akasaka detached palace."

6   I inherited the *netsuke*. These small, often intricately carved wooden or ivory
    ornaments were used originally as toggles for belts but by the late nineteenth
    century often took the form of freestanding sculptures for sale to tourists and
    collectors. See Edmund de Waal, *The Hare with the Amber Eyes*. London, 2010.

7   Charles continued buying books from France after he returned to America.
    When he died his widow, a fervent Presbyterian, arranged for bookplates to be
    placed in all of his bound books. The unbound volumes were all in French. She
    had them burnt.

8   For details of James' career, see Henry Pearson, *James S. Wadsworth of Geneseo*.
    New York, 1913; and Wayne Mahood, *General Wadsworth*. New York, 2002.
    I'm grateful to Professor Mahood for private correspondence about Charles
    Wadsworth.

9   William Wadsworth's descendants built a large house called the Homestead
    at the other end of the village from Hartford House. Until very recently

William's descendants also owned tens of thousands of acres of land in the Genesee valley.

10   See Alden Hatch, *The Wadsworths of the Genesee*. New York, 1959, p. 98.

11   On this period in Paris, see Stephane Kirkland, *Paris Reborn: Napoleon III, Baron Haussmann and the Quest to Build a Modern City*. New York, 2013; and Charles Meryon and Charles Baudelaire, *Paris 1860 : eaux-fortes sur Paris*, Paris, 2002, an evocative pairing of poems and letters by Baudelaire with etchings of Paris by his contemporary Meryon.

12   Charles' letters to his mother dating from his youth to 1866 were glued into a huge leather-bound volume presumably after Charles' father died, because many of the letters from Paris urged his mother not to tell James of the financial troubles that Charles was having. The volume is now in the New York Historical Society library.

13   John F. Krumwiede, *"Old Waddy's Coming": The Military Career of Brigadier James S. Wadsworth*. Baltimore, 2002, p. 24.

14   Lawrence Hewitt, *Port Hudson, a Confederate Bastion in the Mississippi*. Baton Rouge, LA, 1994, pp. 94–95, cites the Wadsworth papers in the New York Historical Society, which I have also consulted. The casualty figure appears in a pencilled note that Charles wrote to his mother under heavy fire on May 22, 1863.

15   On the Burdens, see Louis Auchincloss, *A Voice from Old New York*. New York, 2010, pp. 175 ff. The horseshoe-making machine invented by Burden and patented in 1835 could produce sixty horseshoes a minute. In the Civil War, Confederate cavalry frequently raided Union wagon trains to obtain Burden horseshoes, which were far superior to any produced in the Confederacy.

16   For the text of these two letters, see Pearson, *James Wadsworth*, pp. 246–47.

17   Charles took farming seriously enough to buy several books about it. Two of my favorite titles, which survived at Westerly until it was sold, were *Harris on the Pig* and *Talks on Manure*. The capacious barns and stables at Westerly were built soon after Charles' arrival. See Daniel Fink, *Barns of the Genesee Country, 1790–1915*. Geneseo, NY, 1987, pp. 209–11.

18   Hatch, *The Wadsworths of the Genesee*, p. 100.

19   In 1886, Charles earned the Democratic nomination for the 30th Congressional district covering parts of western New York. He failed to be elected in a year when his brother James, who had served as a Republican Congressman in the seat, had not renominated. James regained the seat in 1892. The *New York Times*, July 31, 1894 describes the Wadsworths as "the feudal barons of Livingston County." The seat has never gone to a Democrat. James' son, also James (1876–1952), held it for many years after serving two terms (1914–1926) as a Senator. See Martin L. Fainsod, *James W. Wadsworth: The Gentleman from New York*. Syracuse, 1975.

20 Geoffrey C. Ward, *A Disposition to be Rich*. New York, 2012, p. 301 quotes an 1890 letter from his great-great grandfather, Ferdinand Ward, the ex-Presbyterian minister in Geneseo: "General Wadsworth had a son who died of delirium tremens in an insane asylum." Ward mistakenly assumes that this was Charles, who had nine years to live and died at home. He cites Hatch, *The Wadsworths of the Genesee*, p. 100, where an anecdote about Charles' nightly visits to the American Hotel in Geneseo "until he dropped unconscious on the bar," while believable, is unfortunately unsourced.

21 By carriage, these trips would have taken at least half an hour each way. Charles and Mary were not especially fervent Episcopalians and he didn't worship with her. For the troubled history of the Presbyterian Church in Geneseo in those days see Ward, *A Disposition to be Rich*, pp. 66–69, 76–80 and 107–8.

CHAPTER 3

A Convent Education, 1909–14

BEFORE BEBO WENT TO BOARDING SCHOOL IN ENGLAND IN 1908 she had only sporadic formal education and, it seems, she had also failed to attract much affection from her nomadic, socially active parents. As the sixth child of eight with two favoured boys born afterwards, she often told me that she received less attention and love as a child than she felt that she deserved. Several plaintive letters to her mother, dated from 1905 and 1906, and addressed to Paris from New York have survived.

Bebo compensated for this situation and edged onto center stage by inventing crises, telling lies and acting up. In 1937 she told a therapist that in her early years she had been "precocious, exhibitionistic, told fantastic tales and early wrote curious verses." She made this self-assessment, to be sure, when she was undergoing a mental crisis and it may be unduly harsh but she enjoyed telling us about the scrapes she had gotten into as a child. In one prank, she pretended to have gone blind and fooled her governess for several hours.

Although Bebo's relationship with Daisy improved once she grew up, it was always problematic because Bebo looked to her mother for approval and affection that seem occasionally to have been insufficient or withheld.

We know less about her relationship with her father, although several playful letters between them have survived, especially after she'd left home to be married. Her quicksilver sense of humor, her straight-forwardness and her skill as a rider must have appealed to him and she boasted to a therapist at Bloomingdale that her father "was subject to terrific temper rages. [I] Could handle him better than [my] Mother—would jolly him out of them."

From 1908 to 1914, a period when her parents were spending much of their time in Europe, Bebo attended Roehampton Sacred Heart Convent, a prestigious Catholic boarding school on the southwestern fringe of London that at the time housed perhaps a hundred girls. The Mothers of the Sacred Heart, a teaching order founded in France in the 1840s, had established it in 1850. Alumnae of Roehampton include President John F Kennedy's sister Kathleen, the actress Vivien Leigh, the novelist Antonia White (see below) and the anthropologist Mary Douglas. Bebo's sister Hester joined her there for a couple of years.[1]

Bebo told therapists in 1937 that her parents at this stage considered her "a liar and incorrigible," but she seems to have accepted Roehampton's multiple restrictions, privileges and routines happily enough to become a good but not outstanding student.

In later life Bebo often spoke about the prudery at the convent and its absurd, fully clothed bathing arrangements whereby girls were never allowed to see their naked bodies.[2] Although she made friends with several nuns and fellow students, none of her student friendships extended into later life—perhaps unsurprisingly, as Bebo seems to have been the only American student at Roehampton once her sister Hester had left.

Apart from the time she spent at a sanatorium in Arizona in 1936 and later at Bloomingdale, Bebo's years at the convent were the most disciplined ones in her life. The routines, rules, privileges and privations were almost numberless. To combat narcissism, there were no mirrors in the convent. To forestall romantic friendships, students could only walk in groups of three or more. The reading of unauthorized texts was not allowed. The girls, almost all of whom were drawn from wealthy families, were being trained to discipline themselves, to be graceful and mannerly and (indirectly) to become good wives and mothers of the privileged class to which most of them belonged. Sex education, of course, was as non-existent at Roehampton as it was for my father before World War I or for me, forty years later, in a secular all-boys boarding school.

The author Airene Botton, two years younger than Bebo, attended Roehampton at the same time and in 1934, using the pseudonym Antonia White, immortalized her time at the convent in her well-received novel *Frost in May*.[3] When the book appeared, as we shall see, it had a strong impact on Bebo, who wrote the convent expressing alarm at the tone of the novel and denying, half-jokingly, that she had written it.

Several of Bebo's letters from Roehampton have survived, along with report cards from 1909 and 1912. The earlier one gives her marks (out of a possible 100) as English 50, French 70, Maths 10, Order 22, Needlework 55, Music 60, Drawing 70, Manners and deportment Good. These strengths and weaknesses (except for the poor mark in English, unless this includes spelling) followed her through her life. In 1912, the results were similar and the report closed with the perceptive notation "very good when she tries."

Most of Bebo's letters from Roehampton are undated and their consistent chirpiness, perhaps demanded by the genre and by the fact that her parents were usually far away, may be deceptive.[4] She probably felt more abandoned than some of her schoolmates whose parents lived nearby and she closed one of her letters to Daisy, at that point living elsewhere in Europe, by saying: "I am very happy though a little lonely and I can perfectly understand that you cannot come over here however I am terribly disappointed."[5] The same letter has a long passage about a three-month-old pet donkey at the school being cared for by the nuns: "He has never been beaten so that nothing in the world frightens him. The nuns groom him and he wears a white flannel jacket at night." The donkey makes a cameo appearance in *Frost in May*.

At the end of 1911 Bebo and Hester spent three months on vacation from Roehampton as guests of a fellow student in Mecklenburg-Schwerin in Germany while Winty was foxhunting in England and Daisy was in a rented Paris apartment that was too small to house their children. In September she wrote Bebo what was probably meant to be a soothing letter: "I am glad you are resigned to a Xmas in Schwerin; I think it will really be pleasanter for everybody as even with doubling up we shall be a bed short in the apartment."

While Bebo was in Germany, Daisy and Winty spent some time at Cliveden, the country home of Winty's Astor cousins. Daisy wrote Bebo from Cliveden almost breathlessly that:

> Country houses seem to me the most wonderful creations
> and the life in them by far the most civilised ever invented
> by man. We have nothing to compare them with in America.
> I suppose it takes centuries to give them the *patine*.

Daisy and Winty celebrated their twenty-fifth anniversary without any of their children on December 11 in Paris at a small dinner where they were joined by their friend "Uncle Henry" Adams. In Schwerin, meanwhile, Bebo and Hester were learning enough German to read the language with pleasure for the rest of their lives.[6]

Whereas "Antonia White" skilfully traced the defiant

emotional and spiritual development of her main character, Nanda, over five years at Roehampton, Bebo's surviving letters and my memories of what she said about the convent suggest that she was happier, more obedient and more conformist than Botton had ever been. Hermione Lee has written that *Frost in May* "points an emergent individual will against a highly formalized discipline of behavior and thought. There is a clash between Nanda's developing aesthetic sense and the restrictive authority of the church".[7] This perceptive analysis doesn't apply to Bebo's experience at the convent where, unlike Aileen Botton, she won few academic prizes, enjoyed herself and never doubted her Catholic faith.[8]

By and large, as she admitted later on, Bebo was slow to grow up. She told therapists in 1937 that her sleepwalking, which began at Roehampton, was usually spurred by nightmares.

The implications of puberty, the pressures of convent life and what she may have seen as the threat of growing up meant that Bebo was sometimes afraid of being "worldly," a term that certainly characterized her parents. In March 1913 Mother Clinton of Roehampton wrote to Daisy that Bebo would be taking her spring vacation in Blaise Castle near Bristol rather than in Paris as previously planned:

> She does not seem to care for the idea of going to Paris. I think with you, that she was somewhat carried off her feet during the Christmas holidays and she told me that she was sure she would meet many frivolous worldly girls in Paris and that she would rather not go there for the present. Gabrielle has had a very good term. She seems to take a very thoughtful view of herself and she is anxious to make the most of her opportunities ... All in all she seems to have turned a corner in her life, which is a deep consolation to us all.[9]

At about this time, Bebo wrote insightfully to Daisy: "I am always *in extremis* about myself—either delighted or despairing. I wonder when I shall be able to realize that I am a very ordinary person after all."

During her summer holiday in 1912 Bebo with her siblings and under Daisy's guidance helped to design and decorate a small Catholic chapel named after St Felicity on the grounds of Sweetbriar. This elegant stucco building, lovingly described in *Autumn in the Valley*, was where my parents were married in 1924. When Daisy was in residence at Sweetbriar, Mass was often celebrated in the chapel twice a week.[10]

Bebo's last year at Roehampton, 1914, is better documented than the preceding ones. In January after attending a dance in Worcester, England, she wrote Daisy that she had "danced with a man who looked like a Negro waiter—turned out to be an Egyptian and shook like an aspen leaf when he danced saying very sorré, awful sorré at each step." A month later, back in school, Bebo wrote a jocular letter in Latin to her father, who was fluent in the language. A few days later she wrote Hester:

> The subject for the literary meeting is "books." I'm not sure if I like it yet or not it will have to be rather matter of fact and Mother Maud can't bear wandering essays, which are the only kind I can write … Two slight cases of scarlet fever here. A good many girl will go home and the school will all be broken up. But as I have had it, I am not afraid for myself. I don't want to leave until the summer. I think it was the devil that disapproved of people living in convents.[11]

Soon afterwards, however, she unexpectedly changed her mind, writing Daisy that "I don't want to go back to Roehampton next year." She gave no reason for her decision and in May she left the school, as she wrote Hester in 1934, "without saying goodbye to anyone" when it was closed temporarily because of the scarlet fever outbreak that she had mentioned. Bebo refused to live in a boarding house selected by the school because, as she told a therapist in 1937, "[I] was a snob and couldn't bear that." Instead, she located a friend in London, decamped with her to Paris and returned to America on her own, reaching Sweetbriar by the end of May. Writing to his friend Amos French, Winty refers to Bebo at this as "t'other—the youngest girl—hard at work with music and sketching."[12]

Notes

1   The school's main building, and eighteenth-century manor house, was severely damaged in World War II. The school was resuscitated in the 1950s as the Woldingham School in Surrey.

2   My cousin Ann Buttrick tells me that these same arrangements were still enforced when she attended Sacred Heart schools as a teenager in the 1940s.

3   See also Antonia White, "A Child of the Five Wounds", in Susan Chitty (ed.), *As Once in May: The Early Autobiography of Antonia White*. London, 1983, pp, 151–62. Chitty is Antonia White's daughter.

4   Ann Buttrick points out (letter January 25, 2012) that students' outgoing and incoming letters were routinely read by nuns before being mailed or given to the students. The knowledge of this surveillance probably reduced the opportunity for Bebo to make any serious complaints.

5   In 1912, Bebo was stranded at Roehampton over a five-day holiday and was the only student left in her dormitory.

6   On the dinner, see French, *Some Letters from Chan*, pp. 49–50. Hester published translations of Rilke's poetry in the prestigious literary journal *Hound and Horn* in 1930 and Bebo published two translations from German in *Commonweal* in 1948.

7   Hermione Lee, introduction to Antonia White, *Strangers*. London, 1980.

8   Writing to Hester from Roehampton on Good Friday 1913, Bebo mentioned receiving an *aspirant* medal "which will be my first step toward fame … I'm really glad I'm getting my medal for Mummy's sake because I feel she is very disgusted with me for unadornment."

9   No information has survived about Bebo's earlier vacation in Paris and her letters suggest that she enjoyed her stay at Blaise Castle, which was then in private hands and has since become a museum.

10   See Chanler, *Autumn in the Valley*, pp. 75–77. For Sunday Mass Daisy travelled to St Mary's in Geneseo, where the Chanlers feudally occupied the front pew. Both churches are still standing. Winty's funeral was celebrated in St Felicity's in 1926, my sister Judie was married to Robert Houston there in 1955, my cousin Elizabeth Chanler married Bruce Chatwin in the chapel ten years later, my son Tom was christened in it in 1972 and my aunt Gertrude Chanler's funeral service was celebrated there in 2000.

11   Bebo once told me that her father sometimes carried a copy of Horace's *Odes* in a pocket.

12   See French, *Some Letters from Chan*, p. 57.

CHAPTER 4

Free Form Years, 1914–20

DAISY AND WINTY SPENT THE WINTER OF 1914–15 IN Washington, DC, where they saw a good deal of the aging but alert Henry Adams, then deeply involved in his research into medieval French music and the cult of the Virgin Mary. In the closing pages of *Roman Spring*, Daisy describes an evening that Bebo, then seventeen, spent with Adams by herself as one of his many honorary "nieces." The passage reads:

> During the meal they chatted cheerily of places and people they had known, and then settled in the low armchairs of the library for the rest of the evening. There was a pause; Uncle Henry leaned back and with his eyes half-closed and his two hands joined at the upturned fingers. Then he began to talk, softly at first as if to himself; then gathering momentum from his surging thoughts, he went on to speak of all that lay on his mind, the mysteries of time and eternity, man and destiny, his aspiration and helplessness. It was all way over her head, but she listened breathless, feeling that something great and wonderful was happening, though she could not understand it, At last he paused and came back to earth, looked at her and said: "Do you know why I have told you all this?" Of course,

she had no answer. "It is because you would not understand a word of it and you will never quote me."[1]

Bebo must have told Daisy what had happened. She remembered the evening and "Uncle Henry" with pleasure for the remainder of her life. A print of a pencil sketch of Henry Adams by John Briggs Potter dated 1914 hung in her bedroom at Westerly.

In November 1914, shortly before going to Washington, Bebo wrote Hester from Sweetbriar: "The weather is bleak & the landscape is dreary & the servants' beds are filled with bedbugs & Giuseppe is leaving us—but we are cheerful withal," adding that not having Daisy at home was "very peaceful."[2]

Another letter written at this time mentions her playing the piano, something I hadn't known about, while a third tells Hester that she is reading *Anna Karenina* "and can think of nothing else. It is more crystallized and leaves a clearer impression than *La Guerre et la Paix*"—a book that she had also read in French translation. The letter closed by saying that her parents were away and that she had taken refuge with friends in the village "so as not to be alone at Sweetbriar and its howling mob of servants."

Bebo spent much of the next ten years living with her parents. Many of her letters from this period are to her sister Hester, who attended classes for a time at Radcliffe College in Cambridge[3] before marrying the Bostonian Edward Pickman (always known as "Pick"), an historian, in Washington in February 1915. Hester was the first of the Chanler siblings to be married and Bebo was a close friend of the couple for the remainder of her life.

On May 20, 1915, celebrating her own eighteenth birthday, she wrote "Dear Mrs P" that "We want you home very badly—to marry us off"—referring to herself, Teddy and her sister Beatrice.

Bebo came into New York society as a debutante in New

York City in December 1916 with her cousin Elizabeth (Libber) Emmett. The *New York Times* of December 7, 1916 mentions a dinner dance in New York City that Bebo attended. When I was preparing this memoir, my cousin Ann Buttrick relayed a scarifying story, told to her by her mother, about Bebo's "coming out": "When Bebo and her cousin Libber Emmett were debutantes they came into a room together, dressed for a ball, and Daisy said to Bebo, "My dear, you look like a potato coming in with a rose." The rest of the year is a blank as far as her letters are concerned.[4]

Seen as a bloc, what I've called the free form years between Bebo's leaving Roehampton at seventeen and getting married ten years later are difficult to deal with because they are poorly documented and because Bebo seems at several points to have lost her bearings to an extent. Neither Roehampton nor her parents (to say nothing of Geneseo) offered a clear path for her to follow. Going to college was never on the cards and although years later she told a psychiatrist perceptively that she "should have taken up something very hard, very young", she didn't, remarking on another occasion that after leaving Roehampton she "had nothing to do for years and much too much liberty. She liked to talk and everyone told her she talked too much. In those days [she] was very fat."

Bebo had no serious beaux (in the wording of the Bloomingdale records, which might be hers, she "scoffed at serious love affairs") and the cheerful tone of her letters to Daisy and Hester in this period may sometimes have been forced although, like almost all her letters, they are fun to read. In April, alone in Sweetbriar, she wrote to Daisy:

> I am enjoying the solitude. One of its chief charms is that there are no servants. How nice it would be if we could live like in the fairy tails [*sic*] and have everything done by

invisible hands! I make my own bed and black my own boots. The servants arrive in an hour and I shall resume my position as the pampered daughter of the idle rich.

She added that her dog Dido has fallen ill and "having no medicine for her I used Christian Science and popish rites."

When the United States declared war on Germany in April 1917, Winty, although in poor health and fifty-four years old, was eager to enlist. Happily, as Daisy put it in her edited collection of his letters:

> The US Commander, General Pershing, asked a friend, General Wright, to find him two good men and true of social and worldly experience, familiar with the language and ways of France, to be his personal aides. General Wright's choice fell on William Cameron Eustis and Winthrop Chanler. So, it happened that these two old friends ... sailed as enlisted men with General Pershing and his staff when these went to France to make arrangements for the forces that were to follow.[5]

Winty had recently been seriously ill and had lost a kidney but going off to war appealed to him and he was impossible to stop. When two of his friends tried to dissuade him from going overseas, "Winty simply laughed at [them] and said it was the greatest piece of luck that had ever come his way."[6] In France he quickly obtained a commission.[7] He spent most of his time as an interpreter for the US general staff in France before seeing action on the Italian front in 1918 where he earned a citation for bravery.[8] He returned home as a major in early 1919. His letters from the war were uniformly informative and joyous. It's hard nowadays to accept the notion of war as an enjoyable adventure but this is how Winty saw it and his experiences, by and large, were "fun". To be sure, he spent very little time in the trenches on the Western Front.[9]

Bebo spent a couple of months in the summer of 1917 visiting her friend Helen Crocker in northern California. She wrote several cheerful letters home about her stay and described a stroll through Chinatown as well some daunting automobile excursions in the redwood country north of San Francisco.[10]

In December, when Bebo and Daisy were in Boston visiting Hester (Pick was away in the Navy), Bebo wrote her father, then in France, about attending a business college where "arrt culturre [*sic*] & beauty are quite dead!"[11] She was taught English and spelling as well as typing, adding, "Mamma has the lowest opinion of the English teacher and sends me to school armed with dictionaries and encyclopaedias to refute everything she says. Poor woman, I pity her." Two years later Bebo completed a full-time secretarial course in Rochester, NY, and earned what she was proud to call her unique diploma.

In 1918, as part of the war effort, she studied motor mechanics in Geneseo. She always enjoyed driving and I see now that a helpful way to describe her life is as a series of successful attempts on her part to master demanding skills such as driving, riding, swimming, tennis, gardening, bridge, painting, embroidery, languages and, in her final years, weaving. Her determination to achieve good results needs to be set alongside what may seem from a twenty-first-century perspective to have been in some ways an idle, directionless life.

That year may also have been when Bebo swam across Conesus Lake near Geneseo (approximately a mile), a feat that she was always pleased about and that would have been impossible once she started smoking. For the closing months of the year, she worked as a typist at the Red Cross headquarters in New York City.

Porter, meanwhile, graduated from St Marks School in Southboro, Massachusetts in 1917 at the head of his class. He entered Harvard in the fall. For a few months in 1918–19 he served in the US Army without going overseas. He returned to graduate from Harvard in 1920, a year early and again at the head of his class, majoring in Classics and Government.[12] He was a member of the University Rifle Team and served as treasurer in the Classical Club. By and large, his years at Harvard, unlike mine thirty-some years later, don't seem to have been much fun. At least, he never recalled them to us with pleasure.

Happily, he enrolled after graduation in Balliol College Oxford, where he spent three fruitful and enjoyable years and became a lifelong Anglophile. He also earned a double first-class degree in law and jurisprudence. He enjoyed telling us of his "interview" for Balliol, when his admission was certainly a foregone conclusion. Asked if he could read Latin, Porter said, "Yes", and the Balliol don replied, "Few Americans can" before closing the interview by advising Porter to dress warmly for the English climate.

Porter's time at Balliol was the happiest stretch of his life so far. It was also relatively unhurried; he had time, as he hadn't had at Harvard, for sport (rowing in an Eight), for making friends and for congenial, harmless college pranks, such as going through an entire day backwards for the Hysteron Proteron (last/first) Society, whose fellow members presented him with a two-headed silver bowl as a wedding present. Other pranks included bringing the largest item beginning with Q into the college (he brought a string attached to Queens College, several blocks away) and bicycling into the countryside to locate the fetid pond from which, it was widely believed, the Balliol kitchen drew its soul.

Notes

1   Chanler, *Roman Spring*, pp. 307–8. For an extended riff on the passage see R.F. Blackmur, *Henry Adams*. New York, 1980, pp. 304–6.

2   I can't identify Giuseppe, but I suspect he was the butler/major domo. Another Italian, Venturino, took his place and worked for the Chanlers until the early 1930s.

3   In a letter to Hester Bebo jokingly referred to Radcliffe as the "Ratcliff Female Seminary". Her brother Hubert, who graduated from the US Naval Academy in 1922, was the only one of Bebo's siblings to earn a tertiary degree.

4   *New York Times*, December 7, 1916 mentions a dinner dance in New York City which Bebo attended. When I was preparing this memoir, my cousin Ann Buttrick relayed a scarifying story, told to her by her mother, about Bebo's "coming out": "When Bebo and her cousin Libba Emmett were debutantes they came into a room together, dressed for a ball, and Daisy said to Bebo, "My dear, you look like a potato coming in with a rose."

5   Margaret Chanler (ed.), *Winthrop Chanler's Letters*. New York, 1949, p. 132. Winty often boasted that when he enlisted, he might well have been, at 54, the oldest private in the US Army.

6   French, *Some Letters from Chan*, p. 69.

7   A 1917 letter from Bebo to Hester notes that a telegram signed "Pershing" approved the commission document (which had been sighted by my cousin, the then Senator James Wadsworth) and "waived the following physical defects and then came a string of Latin names which neither of them could make out at all."

8   On Winty's military activities, see French, *Some Letters from Chan*, pp. 82–3.

9   Many of these letters are reproduced in Chanler, *Autumn in the Valley*, pp. 158–205. See also French, *Some Letters from Chan*, pp. 69–80.

10   Bebo's handwritten journal of this visit, which I recall reading at Westerly in the 1940s, has not survived. Unlike Daisy, Bebo enjoyed the American West, returning there in 1937, 1939 and once in the 1950s.

11   Like many New Yorkers of her background at the time Bebo, her parents and her siblings could not properly pronounce the letter "r" except at the beginning of a word. In writing her father, she was imitating the Geneseo accent, with its strong "r's".

12   I've never discovered Porter's rationale for finishing Harvard in three years.

Porter, London, 1923

CHAPTER 5

New York, Paris and Sweetbriar, 1920–24

IN 1920 BEBO AND PORTER HAD NOT YET ENTERED EACH
other's lives. She spent part of the year studying painting in
New York City. In the spring she was a bridesmaid at her
cousin "Libba" Emmett's wedding to Edwin Morgan. Libba was
Bebo's favourite cousin and served as matron of honor at Bebo's
wedding in 1924.[1] Eddy Morgan, Elizabeth's husband, was an
alcoholic philanderer who sometimes beat her. Libber died of
leukaemia in 1934. According to her nephew Ben La Farge she
also suffered from a broken heart.

Bebo followed her parents to Paris in 1921 on their first visit
there together since before the war. In the spring she travelled
to southern Italy and Sicily with her mother. She found Rome,
which she hadn't visited since 1908, to be a sad revelation. She
wrote her friend Janet Longcope that the Hotel Regina where
she and Daisy stayed was "full of *cocottes* and vulgar people of all
sorts … As for Mummy's old friends: sad tired old people who
are very hard up."[2] In a letter to her brother Teddy soon afterwards, she amplified these remarks, telling him:

You can give up of my ever becoming frivolous—smart society here is much more sickening than it is in N.Y.—they are all drearily immoral—there is no gaiety and for me no glamour at all. Mamma says it isn't a bit the way it used to be. The only people I like are quiet refined dodos who despise society and don't go out at all.

Over Easter she travelled to Florence with Porter, Porter's mother and two of Porter's Oxford friends. There is no indication in the correspondence that anything "clicked" (to use the slang of the period) between Bebo and Porter at the time.

Travelling in southern Italy in August she and Daisy made a side-trip to attend a Mass offered by the allegedly stigmatic priest Padre Pio[3] and on the way north they visited Daisy's friend the art connoisseur and historian Bernard Berenson in his sumptuous villa, I Tatti, outside Florence.[4]

In Paris, Winty and Daisy had rented an apartment on rue Auguste Vacquerie in the 16th *arrondissement* but Winty wrote his friend Amos French in November 1921 that "Bebo is with us but lives on t'other side of the river and works at her painting."[5]

In her last book *Memory Makes Music*, Daisy described the intense musical life that she enjoyed in Paris at that time. She met the composers known as Le Six, played piano four hands with Francis Poulenc and invited the eccentric composer Erik Satie to dinner "several times." At one of these dinners, Daisy's young American friends Gerald and Sara Murphy, accompanied on the piano, sang a selection of Negro spirituals. Satie was pleased by what he heard but suggested that they sing them again with their backs turned with no accompaniment, sensing astutely that *a capella*, and perhaps no white faces, were better settings for the songs.[6]

Daisy also attended innumerable operas and concerts. Bebo

Bebo 1924

remembered seeing a production of Debussy's opera *Pelléas et Mélisande* with Daisy at this time. She enjoyed the evening but the unnerving musical experience left Daisy in "complete bewilderment" and was followed by a sleepless night.[7]

The months that Bebo spent in Paris were probably the most freewheeling ones of her life. On one occasion she attended a (masked?) ball where three or four partners invited her for inno-cent-sounding *rendez-vous*, only to withdraw the invitations one by one (returning to the dance floor, perhaps) when they discov-ered that she wasn't married. Otherwise, it seems, she would have been available to them for an "adventure." Bebo was always amused by this event, so indicative of the double standard that was operating in privileged circles in Paris and elsewhere at the time.

Like Daisy, Bebo was an ardent Francophile. She often spoke to me nostalgically about her time in Paris in 1921–22 and told me once that had she never married she might have enjoyed living there permanently, presumably by herself. This fantasy, never shared with Porter, would have been feasible on her inherited income but I suspect that had she stayed unmarried she would in fact have chosen to live and find work to do in New York City.

Bebo returned to America with her parents in May 1922. Soon afterwards, thanks to machinations by Daisy, the Genesee Valley Hunt was resuscitated and Winty became the Master, an unpaid but demanding post for which he was ideally suited. He performed the task with skill, determination and pleasure until his death in 1926.

Bebo's brother Teddy, then twenty years old, had been admit-ted to Harvard but chose instead to study musical composition with the expatriate Swiss composer Ernest Bloch (1880–1959), first in New Hampshire and then at the recently established Cleveland Institute of Music where Bloch was the inaugural director. Teddy had some trouble settling in and his parents delegated Bebo, then at a loose end, to keep house for him in Cleveland. She did so for the last four months of 1922, and took a temporary job in the Education Department of the Cleveland Museum of Art.

Her letters from Ohio are characteristically cheery but the Bloomingdale papers reveal that she found the interval "a terrible strain" because she sensed a basic instability in Teddy's personality that frightened her at the time and that she thought she might share. She told a doctor in 1937 that Teddy "knew what the abyss was. I had seen it and pulled him out." This sentence probably refers in part to her months in Cleveland and while the nature of the "abyss" is unspecified, it probably involved binge drinking and sexual experimentation on Teddy's part. In later life, he was discreetly bisexual,[8] and after his marriage in 1931 he for the most part kept his drinking under control.

In Cleveland Bebo rose to the unfamiliar challenges of a regular job and keeping house. She cooked what she called "eatable meals" for the first time in her life and enjoyed her work. For $250 she bought a Model T Ford, which she called "a dream that has no diseases" and wrote to Daisy about her busy social life. In November she and Teddy attended a costume ball where she:

> Was rushed by a dreary young man who first asked me to drink with him in the bushes. When I demurred, he evidently thought it wasn't hot stuff enough to suit me so he offered the attractive substitute of drinking upstairs alone—did you ever?

Between January 1920 and December 1933 America was in the grips of Prohibition (the Eighteenth Amendment to the US Constitution). After they were married Bebo and Porter's only sustained quasi-lawlessness was their defiance of this Amendment. Throughout these years, they regularly purchased bootleg liquor, which, unlike selling it, was not a crime. In the early 1930s Bebo was also active in the Women's Organization for National Prohibition Reform, a group that worked hard to get the Eighteenth Amendment repealed. Unfortunately, alcohol was later to play a harmful role in her life.

The same letter to Daisy spoke of Teddy's sobriety, hard work and unexpected fondness for housekeeping. Bebo added proudly:

Did I tell you my name are now painted on the [Cleveland Museum's] Education Dept door? I think I'll have difficulty breaking away but have no intention of staying. As far as I can see it's a pretty poky job—thousands of minute details to be attended to—good for the character but it palls.

Musically, Teddy's months in Cleveland were a success. Bebo wrote her mother "Block [*sic*] nearly went wild with joy (from all accounts) over Teddy's new fugue. He wants a copy of it for the Institute Library as a perfect specimen!"[9]

Bebo was at Sweetbriar for Thanksgiving and after she returned to Cleveland she wrote ruefully to Hester:

Mamma is very tired and helpless without any children at home. I hate to admit it to myself but I see no help for it but for me to live at home all the year round. Papa is no help to her at all in fact he just complicates life, and the running of the house often seems to be too much for her.

In the winter of 1923, Winty and Daisy rented a house at 33 Fifth Avenue in New York City. Bebo studied painting for a time. She also wrote three short articles on contemporary art and sculpture for *Vogue*, telling Hester:

I'm making an honest penny writing *Vogue* articles. I'm not even sure the penny is quite honest because they are so edited and transmogrified into Voguishness that they are hardly mine—but I get $40 a crack which is the price of my soul.[10]

In 1937 she recalled that when she arrived in Manhattan, she "was so tired—had to sleep and sleep and sleep and sleep"—clearly exhausted by the strain of taking care of Teddy and perhaps also uncertain about where she might be headed. When Bebo arrived in New York, Daisy was suffering from an unspecified illness that kept her bedridden for two months. Recalling that Bebo's 1937 statement was made when she was being probed about possible causes of her own illness, I should cite her letter to Daisy from Cleveland in November 1922, where she wrote: "It's funny how absurdly we exaggerated Teddy's problem. All he needed was a touch of home and sympathetic surroundings and he blooms like a rose!"

Later in the year, perhaps encouraged by her work with *Vogue*, she considered the possibility of taking up a career in New York and wrote to Teddy about her plans. Her brother replied that she should follow her natural instincts: "If you'd been born into a practical family you would have been another kind of freak … You have a real instinct or flair for what's original, and you're not that serious … Hester and I are muscle-bound with seriousness."

In the second half of 1923 Bebo spent several months at Sweetbriar while Daisy lingered in Europe. She struggled to untangle her father's financial affairs, had the house redecorated and supervised the construction of new stables. She found Winty's financial insouciance distressing, as she wrote to Hester:

> I go through periods of black despair about the family finances and then recover from them by becoming placidly torpid and philosophical. It is all frightfully irritating and hopeless, but I think my running the whole show has some effect on our respected father. He was sending all his bills to the office [of his trustees, in New York] to be paid without any account being kept at all except for his overdrafts. I keep hurling these ghastly figures at him and I think this acts as a slight check on him.

Toward the close of the letter, after noting that Winty

planned to ship several horses to England for hunting in 1924, she wrote, "He really should be spanked!"

Notes

1   In 1937, three years after Libba's death, Bebo told a therapist that she had been emotionally drawn to Elizabeth, but at the same time she called her cousin a narcissist.

2   The letter was in the cache that my aunt Hester gave me in 1977. Her friend Mrs Longcope must have forwarded it to her.

3   Padre Pio, now St Pio of Pietrecina (1887–1968), a Franciscan priest, was canonized in 2002 after being credited with many miracles and with bearing stigmata on his hands and feet that often bled while he said Mass. See Alexander Stille, "The Strange Victory of Padre Pio", *New York Review of Books*, October 25, 2012.

4   This seems to have have been Bebo's only visit to I Tatti. The Berenson archive contains forty-two letters from Daisy to Berenson (Water Kaiser, email January 12, 2012). In 1922 Bebo stayed at the Villa Medici nearby with her friend Iris Cutting (later Origo, 1903–1988), who subsequently became a world-renowned author.

5   French, *Some Letters from Chan*, p. 91. Writing to Daisy in 1950 Bebo recalled, "We were living at the Villa des Dames with Lady Winifred Elwes as a chaperone." It's not known who "we" were, what the villa was, what role Lady Winifred played or where Bebo studied. She wrote Iris Cutting that she preferred living apart from her parents because as a family "divided we stand, united we fall."

6   Margaret Chanler, *Memory Makes Music*. New York, 1948, pp. 127–40. On the evening with the Murphys, see Elizabeth Shanland, *Theatrical Feast in Paris from Molière to Deneuve*. New York, 1975, p. 71. In the mid-1920s, Teddy was romantically involved for a time with Gerald Murphy's flamboyant older sister Esther. See Lisaa Cohen, *All We Know: Three Lives*. New York, 2012, pp. 50–54.

7   Chanler, *Memory Makes Music*, p. 133. She might have agreed with Nicholas Clifford's mother, who remarked after seeing another performance of *Pelléas* that the only line in the opera that she appreciated was Mélisande's "*Je ne suis pas heureuse ici*" (Nicholas Clifford, email February 2, 2012).

8   Teddy's wife Maria was openly bi-sexual. The marriage, which lasted until Teddy's death, was an affectionate and happy one.

9   The fugue can be found in the Bloch Papers, Sibley Library, Eastman School of
     Music. In Cleveland, Teddy befriended the composer Roger Sessions (1896–
     1985) who was teaching at the Institute. They remained friends, on and off, for
     the remainder of Teddy's life. See Andrea Olmstead, *Roger Sessions*. New York,
     2007.

10   The articles were "The Sculpture of Sudboinin, *Vogue*, March 1, 1923, "The
     Trend of Modern Russian Art", *Vogue*, April 1, 1923 and "The Classic
     Sculpture of John Gregory", *Vogue*, May 16, 1923. In the same letter to Hester
     she adds, "I never want to live anywhere else. I'm sure the Babylonians felt the
     same way about Babylon."

CHAPTER 6

Courtship and Early Years of Marriage, 1924–30

W E KNOW FROM ONE OF BEBO'S LETTERS FROM Cleveland that Porter came there to dinner on one occasion on vacation from Oxford. They had befriended each other in Italy the year before, but there's no evidence that they were as yet romantically involved.

Porter, meanwhile, had come down from Balliol and enrolled in Columbia Law School to study for the New York State Bar examinations. I'm uncertain when he began courting Bebo and none of her letters to him before they married has survived. Once his courtship started, however, it was determined but initially unsuccessful. In August 1923 he had apparently already proposed at least once and had been rejected.[1] Bebo's letter of rejection, if there was one, has not survived but his response to her rejection, in whatever form it had taken, was passionate and straightforward:

> I love you more desperately than words can express—the more so now, when it seems harder (I cannot say "impossible") to gain your consent. I am not in any way your equal, and could never be good enough for you.

Bebo had apparently mentioned her Catholicism as a barrier to marriage as Porter was an Episcopalian but, in his letter, he tried to brush this barrier aside, promising to raise any children they might have as Catholics while reserving the right to remain a Protestant himself. Ironically, as Porter knew perfectly well, Bebo's sisters Laura and Hester were happily married to non-practicing Protestants so the obstacle that Bebo had conjured up was probably intended not to hurt his feelings while keeping him at arms-length. The obstacle in any case was insufficient to dissuade him.

In the fall of 1923, Bebo made the arrangements for the Sweetbriar wedding of her sister Beatrice to Pierre Allegaert. To extend the pleasure of the occasion—for himself, at least—Winty staged a fox hunt that set out from Sweetbriar immediately following the reception.[2]

By the end of the year Bebo was back in New York, working in the advertising section of the *New York Times*. The writer John Jay Chapman, Bebo's uncle by marriage, wrote to suggest that she might seriously consider a career in women's journalism. With hindsight this is an intriguing "road not taken." Four days later Porter wrote to contest a second refused proposal.

Over the years my sister Mary and I often badgered our parents for the details of their courtship. It was difficult for us to attach the word "romance" to either of them but we could see that their companionable marriage, on balance, had been a happy one for them both. In teasing them we thought that the number of Bebo's rejections (she claimed to a therapist in 1937 that there had been six of these) was impressive and so was Porter's persistence. We never discovered what happened to change Bebo's mind. She told a psychiatrist in 1937 that her "subconscious triumphed over her conscious", whatever that means, when she accepted Porter's proposal in March 1924. A July wedding at Sweetbriar was planned.

Porter occasionally baffled people who didn't know him, and even some who did. Edward Pickman, for example, wrote Bebo to congratulate her on her engagement but noted, "I like Porter very much; however, I do not pretend to know him at all as a large part of him doesn't appear on the surface." Porter's mother once remarked that he was "an acquired taste, like olives" and Bebo's high-flying parents, although pleased by the match, may have been hesitant to give Porter their whole-hearted approval. In 2000, Louis Auchincloss closed a letter to me about Bebo by saying:

> I think Mother had a lot to do with her getting married. Your father, brilliant as he was, was inclined to be a bit too scholarly, a bit too academic in his highly accurate but belabored perception of things, and the Winthrop Chanlers were inclined to snigger at what they may have seen as pomposity. I believe Mother once helped her friend by demanding: "Well, whom do you want to marry? Your mother or Porter?"[3]

On the surface Porter was a cerebral, peaceable, ambitious, family-oriented man. He loved Bebo with a totality that may have unnerved her but he disliked the physical display of emotions and scoffed at self-absorption. Like Bebo, he had no respect for feckless spendthrifts like the Astor orphans or scoundrels like his grandfather Charles Wadsworth.[4] He avoided talk about psychology as a discipline and almost never mentioned the life-altering choices he had made, any sufferings that he may have endured or any of his deeper feelings. He loved being a parent, a son, a husband and a landowning Wall Street lawyer. This concatenation of undiscussed attachments made him easy for many people to like and admire but also made him difficult to know.[5]

When Porter was in his early seventies and semi-retired, Susan and I urged him to take notes for an autobiography. The 30-page document that he produced, no longer in my possession, was precise, informative and chronological, like an extended curriculum vitae. It covered his childhood, his academic and legal career, some of his travels and, at some length, his experiences in World War II. There was no sense of a targeted audience for the memoir, which failed to address his relations with his mother and grandmother, for example, his decision to marry Bebo, his non-negotiable fondness for Westerly, his choice of law as a career in the early 1920s or his conversion to Catholicism in 1941. He probably believed with justice that none of these issues was anyone else's business. If his was an examined life, as Bebo's certainly was, he kept the examination to himself.

Nonetheless, in October 1963, to commemorate the fifth anniversary of Bebo's death, Porter wrote and printed a passionate five-page poem dedicated to her memory, entitled "Anniversary Requiem for GC," which he sent to friends and relatives. The poem, which I've kept, exposed the depth of his love for Bebo—he literally thought she was a saint—and included some very moving, lyrical passages that took me (as a fellow poet) by surprise.

In early April 1924, before her engagement was announced, Bebo sailed for Europe to join her mother, who met her ship in Naples. Bebo returned to America at the end of May, and her month-long engagement was announced in early June.

The trip seems to have been planned on the spur of the moment. It's not mentioned in Daisy's memoirs and I hadn't heard of it until May 2010, when I came across three of Bebo's letters in the New York Historical Society written at the time to Porter's mother, along with a letter written to Hester from the SS *Dulio* as it was leaving port:

> I never thanked you for your Christmas present because I was far too busy getting engaged to Porter. I knew your first reaction will be severe shock but you'll get over it and I realise

it's all lovely … I had to go abroad or I would have collapsed with the strain of living alone, working and having the usual chickenfits … It's ALRIGHT.

Before the ship sailed, Bebo hurriedly wrote her other siblings, except Laura and Teddy, who already knew of her upcoming engagement. From the outbound ship on April 4, Bebo composed a leisurely letter to her prospective mother-in-law:

> I have never felt so happy or so sure that I was doing the right thing. Being engaged is like taking a very high dive, awful when you're doing it but it's fine when it's over! I only hope I wasn't too hard on Porter until I made up my mind.

In another letter from the ship she wrote next to Porter's mother, "The other night they told fortunes and I was informed that I was about to marry an old man. Poor Porter!" After the ship docked, Daisy wrote Mary from Naples: "Bebo seems radiantly happy and feels sure she is doing the right thing. She is taking a leaf out of your book and speaks of Porter with tears in her eyes—how unlike her!"

On April 24, Bebo wrote Hester a warm and revealing letter from Naples. Its ink has faded so much as to make it almost unreadable, but it's worth quoting at length.

> Many thanks for your nice letter and the lavish check which I shall squander in Paris. I'm staying on here until Mamma sails and then I go to Paris *alone* for three weeks and then home. It's so difficult to explain one's sudden actions—I just told you the facts and let it go at that! I'm extraordinarily free of chicken fits though I had a whole brood of them in New York. I think life is going to be full of adventures and pleasantness and I think it's great fun to marry someone as young and promising as Porter.

Bebo Washington D.C. 1925

The letter went on to describe Porter's impressive career so far and the couple's plans to live in Washington after the wedding. It closed by saying that she and Daisy were taking local excursions, "coming back to Naples every two or three days for a bath and a rest. There are wonderful things to be seen far off the beaten track."[6]

Bebo was almost twenty-seven at this point. She had probably begun to live with the possibility of never marrying at all. It's clear that she didn't fall in love with Porter to the extent that he fell in love with her. At the same time, she always knew that he was a sound, intelligent, warm-hearted, intensely ethical and very admirable man. In the Bloomingdale papers, the wording about their marriage, perhaps provided by Bebo, was that "they were very happy together, never quarrelled or had a scene."

To be sure, Porter and Bebo had complex, intense and

Bebo Washington D.C. 1925

challenging personalities. They also brought psychological baggage to the marriage that is barely hinted at over the years in their consistently congenial correspondence.

Porter and Bebo were married in St Felicity's chapel on July 8, 1924, a week after Porter had passed his examinations for the New York Bar. Recalling the fox-hunt that had followed Beatrice's wedding, Bebo pleaded successfully with her parents for a smaller party and rejected Winty's jocose proposal to stage some whippet races to follow the reception. His riposte was to give her away in formal clothes as planned, wearing inappropriate brown boots. About fifty guests, all but one of them relations by blood or marriage, attended the wedding. The exception was Porter's best man, his classmate at St Marks School and Harvard room-mate George Gardner Monks, who was then studying for the Episcopalian priesthood. Bebo's favorite aunt Elizabeth Chapman was the only "Astor orphan" who attended, aside from Winty. "Libba" Morgan was Bebo's matron of honor.

Two of Bebo's three sisters were absent—Beatrice because she was pregnant and Hester because she had been committed to a clinic affiliated with Johns Hopkins University in Baltimore, suffering from a nervous breakdown after the birth of her fifth child in nine years.

On his wedding day Porter wrote to his mother, the strongest female influence in his life so far: "I know that no one has ever had such a mother, and I repeat in very childish language that I love you and always will." Over the next three years, before his mother died, Porter wrote her hundreds of happy, informative letters that resembled the ones he wrote Bebo and his children later on.

At Porter's insistence the couple spent their honeymoon in England and Scotland visiting Porter's Balliol friends and some of his English relations. The trip was apparently enjoyable for them both, even though throughout her life Bebo much preferred France and Italy to England.

On July 27, Mother Eyre of Roehampton wrote to congratulate Bebo on her marriage: "I hope so much that Mr Chandler is a Catholic but I suspect you will soon convert him, if not."

The nun was prescient but Porter's conversion to Catholicism in which Bebo played a leading role didn't occur for another seventeen years.

Porter had accepted a position in the Department of Justice in Washington, DC, before the marriage and in September 1924 he and Bebo settled into a furnished two-story, two-bedroom townhouse at 1618 Q St NW that is still standing. Bebo enjoyed moving in and wrote Daisy that she found Washington "very soothing" after New York. She employed two servants and used some of her free time to paint and to shop for antique furniture. At some point she posed for a set of appealing studio photographs.

Bebo and Porter made friends at this time with Dean and Alice Acheson. Like Bebo, Alice was a gifted painter and the two women frequently painted together. Dean, a few years older than Porter, was beginning a long and distinguished legal and government career. He would serve as secretary of state under President Harry Truman.

As usual, Bebo exchanged letters with her parents. Winty wrote her in October after a seven-hour foxhunt to ask en passant how much Porter (whom he inexplicably nicknamed "Piers Ploughman") was being paid.

In this period, Bebo and Porter were concerned about Bebo's sister Hester. Hester's hospitalization in Baltimore for a nervous breakdown had already lasted for a year and no end was in sight. Teddy, who was back in Paris studying under Nadia Boulanger,[7] wrote Bebo that "Pick's letters are heart-rending, without being at all definite" and Laura wrote in November that "Pick's last account was simply tragic," while Porter wrote to his mother, who was fond of Hester, that:

> I hope that poor Hester will soon recover. My impression of her is that she doesn't know how to *stop thinking* for a single

minute. Her mind is never at rest and the perfectly natural result is a complete mental breakdown. Poor Bebo has again paid the penalty for being capable.

Toward the end of 1924, Bebo prepared what she wrote to Hester was an "oppulent" [*sic*] Thanksgiving dinner in the Q Street house for Porter, Hester's husband Edward Pickman and Porter's mother. She was pleased to report that "Porter made a punch out of everything we had in the house which wasn't much but the result was quite intoxicating." The next day, she and "Pick" visited the newly completed Lincoln Memorial. Bebo thought that the "*coup d'oeil* [was] magnificent" but she found the statue of Lincoln "very hideous." She closed by saying that "It is so nice to have [Pick], as I am alone all day so I hope he'll come often when he's seeing you."

Hester replied that she wished she had attended the dinner. She remained in the clinic for three more months. Bebo told a therapist in 1937 that Pick's hair turned "grey with worry" while Hester was in the hospital. He had no way of knowing, of course, whether she would ever emerge or regain her health.

For most of 1925 Bebo and Porter were in Washington exchanging letters with their parents. Winty had developed a teasing relationship with his newest son-in-law and wrote him from England that after meeting several lawyers that "I have become so legal I can't spit straight," while Porter, writing to his mother in July, told her that "Bebo and I saw the Ku Klux Klan parade yesterday afternoon and grew very despondent. There were about 20,000 of the stupidest faces I have ever seen."[8] In the same summer, Bebo later recalled watching a parade of Shriners, a fraternal order that favored "Oriental" costumes. As she watched, hundreds of the marchers' ornamental slippers came off into the melted asphalt.

At the end of 1925 Bebo and Porter moved to New York City, where they rented an apartment at 129 East 82nd Street that was "sunny, high up and with a fireplace", as Bebo wrote to Winty, while Porter worked in the US District Attorney's office for the next two years.[9] Bebo and Porter hired a young Irish woman, Angela Lombard, to work for them in an undefined capacity. Ms Lombard returned to the family in 1934 as a governess. She was still alive in 1977 when Susan and I visited New York and we engaged her briefly as a baby sitter.

In March Bebo wrote Daisy about a mutual friend named Ethel Derby, a daughter of Theodore Roosevelt who had been a friend of Henry Adams:

> Her danger is to become too uplift [*sic*] it's a shame. She's deliberately crushing her critical sense in order to convince herself that everything is bright and beautiful. I think she thinks I'm a Cassandra. I don't dare tell her about the priest who said that it wasn't uncharitable to call a man a fool if he was one.

The context for this letter is unclear but Bebo, without ever being a pessimist, always distrusted Pollyannas. She had a rare capacity, noticed by many of her friends, to assess the *chiaroscuro* of any situation. This meant that she could often see the tragic, saintly, inept, appealing, false and comical aspects of a person's character in a flash. Because of this talent, or curse, the world sometimes broke against her like surf and after she died Louis Auchincloss wrote Porter to say that in a metaphorical sense she had "no eyelids". In a similar vein, a therapist noted in 1937 that "[She] believes that it is because of her acute intuition that she knows more about people than they will admit to themselves. This at times leads her to be very tactless."

In the summer of 1926, Winty Chanler suffered a stroke

while riding near Sweetbriar with his wife. He fell from his horse, went into a coma and died a month later. He was sixty-three and had been in poor health for several years. His death left Daisy a widow after nearly forty years of marriage.

Winty had never been interested in religion and described himself jokingly as a Free Will Baptist exercising his free will on Sundays by not going to church, but he was respectful of Daisy's religious faith and occasionally attended Mass with her. To please Daisy, he always claimed that he would become a Catholic when his head was half an inch from the ground on his final fall from a horse. Daisy took his promise literally and arranged for Winty, in semi-consciousness, to be baptized a Catholic. He was buried in the Catholic cemetery in Geneseo after his anti-Catholic siblings, angered by his conversion, refused to allow him to be buried in the Chanler family vault in Trinity Church in New York City.

Although none of Bebo's surviving letters mentions it, she was pregnant for most of 1926 and in late December she gave birth to a healthy boy, to be named John, who died a few hours later from complications connected with his breech delivery. I had always understood that the baby was christened a Catholic and I was surprised to discover when I visited Geneseo in 2010 that his body is buried in the Protestant cemetery alongside Porter's parents.

I've often thought, as I know Bebo often did, how different our family history and dynamics might have been had the baby lived. Porter and Bebo were devastated by the loss and soon afterwards, according to the Bloomingdale records, Bebo began to sleepwalk and hallucinate, something she hadn't done since she was a teenager at Roehampton. She and Porter received more than forty letters of condolence. Hester wrote: "Everyone who has been through what you have says there is nothing so desolate and hard to face as the weeks of idle convalescence that you have ahead of you." Pick's letter caught what he sensed was his sister-in-law's desperate mood. "Dear old Bebo," he wrote,

> I am terribly sorry to hear of your bad luck. There are times in all our lives when something happens which turns the whole world yellow and brutal. I had it when Hester took up what seemed for a time to be an indefinite stay at Johns Hopkins.

A year later, when Bebo had recovered somewhat, Priscilla Auchincloss was confident about her future:

> What deep waters you have had to go through this last year but you must not let it shake your confidence in life too completely … I have watched you grow in wisdom and know you can know cope with anything.

Porter and Bebo travelled to Bermuda in January 1927 and in February, back in New York, Bebo wrote Daisy a vivid description of a dinner party organized by her sister Laura "that started out very high-brow and ended up by being rather a mess." Bebo sat next to the Italian son of an old friend of Daisy's

> who was too Roman and generally Latin for the party—he is nice but altogether too concentrated on perpetual experiments on Woman with a capital "W." The material he had to work with was distinctly unpromising—Aileen Tone, Frances Livingston, Laura and I. It was comic to see him work so hard for a flirtatious reaction.

In those days Porter was considering working in a law firm in Buffalo that was within relatively easy reach of Geneseo. In the aftermath of John's death, however, as Bebo wrote Daisy in March, he agreed to postpone the move. She added: "I don't feel I'm up to anything quite as desolate [as Buffalo] just yet." They lingered in New York City for another year.

Bebo miscarried in October 1927, according to the Bloomingdale records, but her letters fail to mention this. Instead, they are consistently cheerful except when they concern the death of Porter's mother from intestinal cancer, which also occurred in October, when Mary was sixty-one. After a party in New York in February 1928, Bebo wrote chirpily to Daisy:

> I was just a little drunk and very carefree and danced until 3—which I hardly ever did even as a deb. Porter was more than a little drunk and loosened up no end. If he once got a taste for dissipation there's no telling where it will take him.

That summer, Porter and Bebo hosted a wedding reception for Porter's cousin William Wadsworth and Martha Schofield. Up until then, their house had no name. They chose to call it "Westerly" for the invitations. As the reception wore on, several church-going ladies from Geneseo, active in the temperance movement, were loosened up by a strong punch unidentified as alcoholic. Their impromptu dancing was recorded in a home movie and when the reception ended one of their cars ran into a Westerly gatepost. On the following morning, a Sunday, Porter and Bebo were condemned by name from the pulpit of the Presbyterian Church in Geneseo, where Jessie Wadsworth had worshipped for many years. Their offence had been to serve alcohol in the heyday of Prohibition and thereby to deceive some of the parishioners.

A few months later, Bebo and Porter moved to Buffalo after all. They lived there for a year. In December at Bebo's suggestion they adopted a six-month-old baby who was christened Joseph Redfield Chandler and nicknamed Joe. Somewhat to her surprise, Bebo bonded with the baby and wrote to Daisy that he had a "look of real intelligence" even though she was not "particularly drawn to babies in general." She also found that he looked

"strangely family and not at all an outsider." In another letter she
wrote Daisy that "as long as he is handsome and intelligent, he's
bound to please you."

The unfamiliar strain of motherhood, combined with the
loss of John, what Bebo considered to be the social bleakness of
Buffalo, and her recent miscarriages weighed on her, however, and
she wrote Daisy toward the end of 1928 that "I still feel sensitive
and on the verge of tears at times but I expect I'll soon get over it."

In January 1929 she travelled with a female friend to Aiken,
SC, a fashionable resort, where she "rode all morning and played
tennis all afternoon." By and large, however, she didn't enjoy it.
She wrote as much to Teddy, who replied:

> You must have given the crowd at Aiken a good earful. I can
> see you yawning at them and telling them how dull their vices
> are. Anyhow you sound as if you had a good time "loathing"
> the place.

Happily, for Bebo's morale and Porter's career, the Buffalo
interlude was brief. In September 1929, Porter accepted a position
at the Wall Street law firm of Davis, Polk, Wardwell, Sunderland
and Reid, one of the top law firms in the city. He worked there
happily until a couple of years before he died, specializing in
corporate litigation.[10]

In October 1929, a month after Porter joined the firm, the
so-called Wall Street Crash set off the Great Depression. Bebo
and Porter were insulated from the disaster by their private
incomes and because the turmoil brought a great deal of prof-
itable business to Davis Polk although Bebo told me, perhaps
inaccurately, of losing $20,000 of her inheritance "in a single day."

Once Bebo and Porter were back in New York for good they
established a routine that lasted through the 1930s whereby Bebo
spent from late May to mid-October at Westerly, where she

managed the farm and the estate. Porter joined her for occasional weekends and for a longer holiday in the foxhunting season in September and October. Travel from New York on night trains took about eight hours each way. This meant that on weekends through 1952 or so Porter would normally arrive in Westerly for lunch on Saturday. He would have to leave on Sunday in the late afternoon.

Although she missed her friends and her busy social life in New York City, Bebo seems to have been happy enough with these long, mostly solitary summers. Running the estate and managing the hired staff was a challenging job that she did well. What's more, the summers were less burdensome for her as long as Daisy was at Sweetbriar, only a few miles away.

Whereas Sweetbriar was on the outskirts of the village of Geneseo, Westerly stood by itself on a slight rise three miles from the town. Its isolation grated on Bebo, but the times he spent in the house exhilarated Porter, who identified himself closely with Westerly and the surrounding farm.[11] For him, life on the estate was a soothing, perhaps even Arcadian contrast to his intense, competitive professional life and an assertion of something that Bebo and I and my sister Mary, as social animals, always found enigmatic. When he was in Westerly, Porter became less engaged, lower key and more backward-looking. He seemed happier, if less alert, than he was in the city. The intensity of his feelings about the house and where the feelings sprang from were impossible to penetrate and he never brought them to the surface as something to discuss. Instead, Westerly provided him with a non-negotiable *raison d'être*, oddly similar to his deep religious faith, which was also immune from questioning or discussion.

Notes

1   Interestingly, Bebo's letters to Daisy and Hester in July and August 1923 say nothing about this correspondence, which Porter may well have culled from his papers before donating almost all of them to the New York Historical Society.

2   See Chanler, *Autumn in the Valley*, p. 208; and Thomas, *The Astor Orphans*, p. 272.

3   Louis Auchincloss, letter of August 8, 2000. In his memoir, *A Voice from Old New York*, p. 32, Auchincloss refers to an unnamed friend "whose marriage [Priscilla, his mother] arranged in a difficult situation" and on p. 192 he writes of "one woman who suffered from her mother's opposition to her perfectly acceptable beau, a problem solved by [Priscilla]."

4   Porter inscribed the copy of Lately Thomas's *A Pride of Lions*, which he gave Susan and me for Christmas in 1971: "In the hope that your children will be careful not to grow up like some of these [Astor orphans]." So far, so good.

5   In February 1931, Daisy wrote Bebo from Washington, DC that in an encounter with the distinguished attorney Edward Burling "[He] asked me … if I realized what a remarkable young man I had for a son in law, meaning Porter, and wanted to know what I thought of him. When I said that what I thought particularly noteworthy in him was that he was a good lawyer and one of the best people I had known, Burling couldn't make out what I meant. That is apparently a thing one could not say about a lawyer." In her novel *The Death of the Orange Trees* (New York, 1963), my cousin by marriage Claire Nicolas White unfairly presented a character named "Uncle Schuyler", clearly modelled on Porter, as a tedious stuffed shirt.

6   She probably visited Teddy in Paris and may have come back to America with him as he attended her wedding in Geneseo in July. On his return to the United States Teddy smuggled in a copy of James Joyce's banned novel *Ulysses* to give to his friend the composer Roger Sessions. See Olmstead, *Roger Sessions*. p. 173.

7   Nadia Boulanger (1887–1979) was a French composer, conductor and teacher who taught and inspired many twentieth-century composers, including Samuel Barber, Aaron Copland, Roy Harris, Walter Piston and Philip Glass. In 1962 she presided over a memorial concert of Teddy's music staged in his honor at the Museum of Modern Art.

8   Nicholas Clifford (email, May 4, 2012) writes of this passage: "The Klan was a big deal in the 1920s, [and] North of the Mason Dixon line (including even Vermont! And especially Maine) it was primarily anti-Catholic and generally anti-immigrant. The question of how to deal with the Klan hung up the Democratic Convention of 1924 for days—that was when the Solid South was still Democratic."

9   The apartment was across the street from the one at 108 that Bebo rented in 1942–46.

10 For an admiring account of Porter's legal career at Davis Polk, see John Rousmaniere, *Davis Polk & Wardwell: To the Modern Era.* New York, n.d., a privately printed history of the firm, Chapter 10, pp. 28–31. The firm dropped the commas in its letterhead at some point in the 1940s. I'm grateful to Peter Judd for locating parts of this book on my behalf.

11 The farm, covering some 1500 acres of fertile flatland on the banks of the Genesee River, was rented, and a tenant family lived in the farmhouse where Porter had grown up. Throughout his life, Porter followed details of the farm assiduously.

Bebo New York city, 1932

CHAPTER 7

The Early 1930s:
A Pleasing Family Life

IN 1930 AND 1931 BEBO AND PORTER WERE HAPPILY SETTLED with their baby son, a governess, a maid and a cook in an apartment at 130 East End Avenue in New York City. Bebo and Porter vacationed in Nassau in January 1930[1] and in these years Bebo rented a studio that she shared with her sister Laura, while Porter often worked until midnight or later as companies that were clients of Davis Polk fell into bankruptcy, receivership and dissolution.

Until the 1950s Bebo was an unreflective Republican and like Daisy she took little interest in political issues. Nonetheless, at one point in 1931 she wrote her mother teasingly that she had had been to a party where she had met some "nearly intelligent people who talked cosmically enough about politics to interest you." She was passionately opposed to Prohibition, which she saw as an infringement of personal freedom, and she became chair of Livingston County unit of the Women's Organization for National Prohibition Reform in 1931. The move marked the first of several ventures on her part into the margins of public life.

In March 1932 she wrote to Daisy that her friend Alida

Conover, a painter and illustrator who made her living from her work and was very poor throughout the 1930s

> is being more agin [*sic*] the government every day. She is full of anti-capitalist ideas and laps up anything along that line. She has a funny stubborn streak. I think she hates more than she loves, which is stultifying.

In the early 1930s Porter and Bebo were eager to complete their family and in May 1932 they finalized the adoption of a three-year old girl, Judie, who was a year younger than Joe and came to live in Geneseo that summer.[2] In the same month, as fate would have it, Bebo became unexpectedly pregnant with me. In the fall of 1932, she and Porter and their two children moved from East End Avenue to a spacious twelfth floor apartment at 320 East 72nd Street, where they lived until Porter went off to war a decade later.

Once she learned that she was pregnant Bebo wrote her friend Alma Morgan that she had "mixed feelings" about it, and perhaps about the family of three children that she would soon be responsible for, but Alma replied, "If you dare to have eight after all you've said about Laura [who had just given birth to her eighth child] then I'm through with you!"

In the summer of 1932 Bebo set up an anti-Prohibition booth at the Livingston County Fair in Caledonia, NY, and another at the Rochester Horse Show. In September she attended a two-day New York state meeting of the Women's Organization for National Prohibition Reform in Corning, NY. The organization had more than 600,000 members nationally. Bebo reported to the meeting that she had canvassed 2000 homes about Prohibition and gained 750 signatures supporting repeal.[3]

In early October she took to her bed on doctor's orders to avoid a miscarriage and continued this regime when she returned to New York. From Geneseo she wrote Porter:

Bebo New York city, 1932

The secrecy business [re her pregnancy] is quite hopeless. I'm afraid you ought just as well to tell everybody. I was deluged with invitations this morning and my excuses ran out so think I'll tell Mummy tonight & then it will be all over town! You might call [Laura] at St James. I'm sure she'll be surprised.

I was born on February 7, 1933 (Charles Dickens' birthday) and was named after Ralph Chandler's naval patron, Admiral David Porter, as my father and his father both had been.

Amid the Depression, Daisy continued to lead a cosseted, expensive life but at some point she apparently cut the wages of her domestic staff. In March 1933, just before she embarked for her annual visit to Edith Wharton's villa in France, she wrote Bebo that she was travelling "with three servants [who] are happy to accept the new wage schedule and seem happy to look forward to another summer at Sweetbriar."[4]

Bebo replied that the Sweetbriar staff of nine cost a total of $415 per month or more than $5000 in today's dollars and were too high an expense for Daisy's income even though none of the staff was paid more than $75 a month.

There's no evidence that Daisy made drastic cuts in her staff but after 1934 she stopped travelling to Europe and for the rest of the decade she spent her winters in rented houses and apartments in Washington, DC.

In comparison, Westerly in those years had a staff of five: a cook, two maids, a governess and a gardener-groom,[5] which sounds extravagant but the house was large and the surrounding grounds, gardens and the horses required attention and there were almost no labor-saving devices.

Laura's husband Larry's architectural work at Mc Kim, Mead and White had boomed in the 1920s but was now, as Bebo wrote Hester, "dead as dead." Saving money for the Whites meant closing a large rented New York apartment and cutting back the family's expenses. Larry stayed behind with his mother in her house in the city and in the summer commuted from Long Island, where Box Hill, the spacious house outside St James designed by Stanford White, didn't come into his hands until 1938. Bebo helped to pack up the Whites' New York apartment.[6]

When Daisy was in Europe, Laura wrote Bebo from Germany, where she was living with her children to save money, that Daisy, whom she'd gone to see in Paris:

> Doesn't want to stay away from her family but she hates America … We only had one little argument—which I couldn't resist. She began abusing America. I said that all the nicest people were Americans and included all her best friends! To say nothing of her children and herself!

On May 1, 1933 (May Day) the radical Catholic activist Dorothy Day (1897–1980) and the Catholic anarchist Peter Maurin founded the Catholic Worker movement in New York City. Porter and Bebo, despite or perhaps partly because of their inherited social position, supported the movement enthusiastically from the start.[7] Bebo soon befriended Dorothy, a woman of her own age who possessed enormous spiritual force and who was to write an eloquent eulogy for Bebo in the *Catholic Worker* in 1958. For Bebo, the chance to roll up her sleeves and work for a worthwhile Christian project was a new and rewarding challenge. For my parents, Dorothy's Christianity trumped her Marxism and Porter, who was as devout a Christian as Bebo, was happy to lend a hand.[8]

Bebo paid the first year's rent on the movement's apartment, sometimes helped out in its soup kitchen, and Porter loaned Dorothy the Chandlers' car so that she could look for rural properties where some of the movement's members could live communally and support themselves with agricultural pursuits.[9] In the 1970s Dorothy told an interviewer, "Bebo did all the dirty work for the movement in that first year."

Bebo in these years was subject to bouts of depression perhaps intensified by the ordeals of childbirth and child raising, which began to close in on her after my sister Mary's birth in

1935. She wrote to Teddy about one of these bouts, he chided her in a friendly way and told her to lift her spirits: "Sorry to hear that you're so sick of yourself. Mama always says 'There's *nobody* who can be such wonderful *company* as Bebo. I *defy* anyone to be bored by her!'"

To escape from the city, Bebo spent much of the summer of 1933 in a rented "cottage" in the seaside village of Nonquit, Massachusetts, in order "to get better" and also to cut back on the expenses of living in Westerly. With hindsight, this "cure" may have been worse than the disease.

Because she was separated temporarily from Porter, however, a good run of letters between them has survived. They show that their marriage was at a cozy, companionable stage. She closed one letter, for example, by saying that "I felt sad at you having go back to New York on a Sunday which shows I'm feeling better or you are more attractive." Three children, a cook, a maid and a governess shared the "cottage" with her. The summer was made more hectic by my *modus operandi*:

> This is a lovely place except that the house is a matchbox and you hear every sound. David turns up at 5 AM and there is no peace until the children get off to the beach at 10 o'clock.

Since 1915 and 1916, respectively, Bebo had observed her sisters Hester and Laura enmeshed in happy marriages that produced eight children for Laura and six for Hester. The youngest children of these marriages were born in 1932 and 1933 and in her letters Bebo was quick to comment, jokingly I hope, on my innate superiority to them both. Visiting the Pickmans in Bedford, Massachusetts, Bebo wrote that her new niece Deborah, born in March, "is lovely but not nearly as important looking as David." As things turned out, Ann White (later Buttrick, 1932–) and Deborah Pickman (later Clifford, 1933–2007) became my lifelong friends.

Bebo self portrait pencil sketch c1933

In another letter to Porter, Bebo urged him to arrive at Nonquit with a cocktail shaker and some family silverware because the "10 cent store" cutlery that came with the cottage had embarrassed the cook. "She's so ashamed of it," Bebo wrote, "She'd rather have the extra work of polishing real silver!" She added: "I miss you very much as I haven't had an intelligent adult to talk to since I've been here." She closed by warning him that "I'm worried about your getting any sleep here. The only hours for sleep are between 9 PM and 5 AM."

Daisy's well-meaning visit later in the summer was an additional strain. Bebo found that she was "forced into constant entertainment ... Mrs Perkins the wife of the president of the National City Bank is coming to lunch. Can you beat it?" Happily, there were also fewer demanding people in Nonquit whom Bebo knew from New York and Washington. She wrote

Porter that "I think I am really all right now as I feel quite ambitious socially which I haven't felt for a long time & I'll pull you along with me."

Bebo's exhausting summer ended in September when she and Porter embarked on a month-long trip to Bulgaria, Greece and Istanbul that they had planned for some time. They chose this itinerary because they shared an interest in Byzantine Christendom and because their friend Jock Balfour, a British diplomat, whom they had befriended in Washington in the 1920s, was stationed in Sofia.[10]

Their three young children, minded by a governess, a housekeeper and a cook stayed in Westerly, a few miles away from Daisy. In Bloomingdale four years later, Bebo mentioned having had nightmares in Istanbul, but she and Porter often recalled the trip with pleasure. They didn't get back to Europe until the summer of 1950.

In the fall of 1933 Bebo spent a few days at Sweetbriar, taking a break from the children, but wrote Porter in New York that:

> I love my own home now that I've had a few days rest & want to get back to it. There is an atmosphere of unreality about Sweetbriar that is only soothing when one is very tired and then [it becomes] slightly irritating.

Once back in the city and settled comfortably into their new apartment on 72nd Street, Bebo continued her sponsorship of the Catholic Worker movement. She was also invited onto the advisory committee of the newly formed Museum of Modern Art (MOMA) alongside Nelson Rockefeller, George Gershwin and eighteen others. The grounds for her being on the committee are unclear and her duties don't seem to have been very demanding.[11] In May 1939, she and Porter hosted a dinner (one of forty such dinners in New York City that night) to celebrate the opening of the building for MOMA. Her connection with the museum seems to have lapsed in the 1940s.

She and Porter were insulated from the Depression but economic conditions for most Americans continued to be grim and in May Bebo's friend Alida Conover wrote her: "More and more I long for a communistic society." Conover, incidentally, was the only one of Bebo's friends—aside from Dorothy Day and her pious entourage—who was genuinely poor in the Depression.

Two books appeared in 1934 that meant a great deal to Bebo. These were Daisy's memoir *Roman Spring* and Antonia White's novel about Roehampton, *Frost in May*. Bebo was quick to recognize that Roehampton was the convent that White called "Lippington." She wrote Hester that the book "made me absolutely and completely sick." She recognized many incidents and lightly disguised characters from her time at the school and she wrote to Roehampton about her strong reaction to the book. As she wrote Hester: "I think you can't say that any of it isn't true, exactly—but the light heartedness and gaiety is all left out which made its joy."

Mother Archer-Shea, still at Roehampton, remembered Bebo fondly and wrote her a comforting letter (which Bebo, writing to Hester, called "extraordinarily broad minded") saying that the "author's real name was Airene Botton. She has now given up her religion." Mother Archer-Shea referred to Botton as "very clever" but after tentatively identifying some of the students in the book she closed the letter by saying that Roehampton was taking no legal action.[12]

After finding out the identity of "Antonia White" Bebo wrote Hester that she had "hated" Botton but gave no details. The novel contains no American characters, although Bebo added that she thought she recognised herself, to an extent, in the heroine.

Daisy's memoir *Roman Spring*, covering her childhood and the first twenty years of her marriage, was scheduled for publication in the fall. In the summer, Bebo wrote Porter from Geneseo:

> The salesman for Little, Brown, Mummy's publisher was at
> Sweetbriar for dinner last night, He was 100% live wire and
> perfectly killing. A dynamo of energy. He showed us the
> confidential notes on the book—full of "pep" talk to the effect
> that *Roman Spring* would be the fashionable book of the year
> as it appealed to both Catholics and social climbers as well as
> all recognized society leaders—don't you love it?

Sales for *Roman Spring* were good and the book was on the *New York Times* bestseller list for several weeks although some of Daisy's in-laws took issue with what they considered her cavalier treatment of Rokeby and the Astor orphans.[13] Bebo's aunt Elizabeth Chapman, for example, in a letter to Bebo, accused Daisy of having "the hide of a rhinoceros and no heart" and added "There's so much that is fine in [the book] that one stumbles involuntarily over the rolling stones, utterly surprised and indignant!"[14]

That summer, Bebo and Porter decided to buy a miniature poodle. Porter had located a mixed litter of them in New York and Bebo sent him a telegram, which failed to reach him and a special delivery postcard from Geneseo:

> Your letter just received. I incline to the black puppy. I mistrust
> all you say about the brown. Browns are freaks and hardly ever
> have brown pups also a white patch means she isn't pure bred.
> I would rather have the intelligent looking black puppy. The
> only dog who ever bit me was a brown poodle.

In the aftermath of the postcard Bebo wrote Porter more calmly:

> A telegram sent in re the poodles was reported not delivered as

you were away. I think this is very annoying. Now your letter
saying you bought the brown poodle comes this morning so
I suppose it's all right. A poodle must have a 'significant eye'.
I do hope the brown one isn't stupid. I don't like brown ones
as a rule but this one might be an exception.

She soon became reconciled to the new poodle, Chocolat,
writing Porter that it "has adopted David as his friend & they
walk across the lawn together, C. constantly knocking David
down who doesn't mind a bit."

Driving at one point that summer from New York to
Geneseo—"lovely country all the way"—Bebo wrote Porter:

I miss you very much when I get home from one of these
jaunts & wish there were some way that we could arrange the
summers more satisfactorily. But you probably prefer your
manly independence!

Bebo devoted much of the summer of 1934 to her painting, producing an impressive, somewhat unsettling self-portrait
that hung in Westerly for many years and an elegant portrait of
Judie that hung nearby. For a studio she used what had been the
icehouse attached to the barns at Westerly, renovated to include
floor-to-ceiling windows. One of the walls was hung with *tapa*
cloth brought back by Ralph Chandler from his time in the
South Pacific in the 1870s.

Bebo's teenaged niece Alida White visited Westerly at this
time and helped Bebo to preserve vegetables from the garden
that could be called on in the winter in the city in an era before
frozen food. As Bebo wrote Porter:

We're canning and canning and canning. I dreamt last night
that there were barrels and barrels full of glass canning jars
from your grandmother's day. Asked James Johnson [the

African-American gardener-groom who worked at Westerly from 1922 until his death in 1950] about them and he says there had been barrels and barrels but your mother had them all dumped in the river.

The bottled ("canned") fruits and vegetables were taken to New York City from Geneseo in a pick-up truck on several occasions before World War II.

At some point in this busy, happy summer, Bebo became pregnant again and on May 24, 1935, my sister Mary Wadsworth Chandler, named after Porter's mother, was born in New York City. Soon after the birth, Dorothy Day wrote Bebo:

> I was so happy to hear the news when I came back this morning. Both happy and envious. You know it was having my Tamar that really brought me into the church. I was so overwhelmed with joy and thanksgiving at this miraculous thing that had taken place.

In closing she asked Bebo to "thank Mr Chandler" for helping the Catholic Worker movement recently by paying several of its bills.

Mary's birth was apparently followed by a bout of depression for Bebo, as Daisy wrote to her in mid-June, using religious imagery: "I am heartbroken to hear that you are less well. There is evidently some poison lurking in your system that must be exorcised."

Daisy, for her part, had begun writing a sequel to *Roman Spring* that was to be called *Autumn in the Valley*. In the pages dealing with the summer of 1935 Bebo appeared anonymously in the book, just as Daisy was writing about riding horses for thirty years in the fields and woods of the Genesee valley:

> As I write, my daughter comes in, flushed with the joy of a forty-five-minute run. "And oh, Mummy, it was so beautiful.

We were galloping as fast as we could and yet I couldn't forget how lovely the whole picture was."[15]

What appear with hindsight to have been Bebo's perennial rheumatism and nerviness flared up that fall and she wrote Daisy that "when I get back [to New York City] end of October I shall probably have to go out to Arizona or New Mexico for a month to bake the germs out of me in preparation for the winter." It's uncertain if some of her worries were connected with an undocumented depression following my sister Mary's birth. In any case, the next two years were traumatic ones for Bebo and her family.

Notes

1   They came home by train, via Florida, which Bebo, writing to Daisy, found "so godawful that we both became anti-American."

2   My daughter Maggie has asked if Judie came to the family with that name. I have no answer for this, but her middle name, Marion, was a Chanler family name and may have been added to an original "Judie" after the adoption. Bebo probably chose the name in memory of her recently deceased, mentally disabled brother, Marion Chanler (1895–1931).

3   Her report was cited in the *New York Times*, November 11, 1932. See also Grace C. Root, *Women and Repeal*. New York, 1934, p. 61. After reading this passage A.W. McCoy wrote (email January 15, 2015): "I suspect that this campaign was seminal in letting cosseted society women into the public sphere for more active lives."

4   At Wharton's villa in 1933 Daisy heard her friend read aloud from the manuscript of her forthcoming memoir.

5   In those days and well into the 1960s there were always two or three horses stabled at Westerly.

6   I'm grateful to my cousins Ann Buttrick, Alida Hare and Cynthia Jay for this information.

7   For a perceptive history of the Catholic Worker movement, see William D. Miller, *Dorothy Day: A Biography*, New York, 1982. See also Dwight McDonald, "The Foolish Things of the World: Dorothy Day", *New Yorker*, October 4 and 11, 1952.

8   When they were students at Harvard Porter and his roommate Gardner Monks had been active in Episcopalian-sponsored social work in Boston.

9   Dorothy Day, *Catholic Worker*, October 1959: "When we looked for our first communal farm, we borrowed Mrs. Porter Chandler's car and canvassed New Jersey and eastern Pennsylvania for months, and with Big Dan driving for us, I was praying to his and the car's guardian angel every time they went out." See also Miller, *Dorothy Day*, p. 292.

10   In a July 17 letter to Hester, Bebo wrote, "Porter says unless he goes abroad, they'll telegraph for him to come back to work after he's been here a day or two as they did last year."

11   Her association with the advisory committee dated back to 1930. See Nicholas Fox Weber, *Patron Saints: Three Rebels who Opened America up to Modern Art, 1928–1943*. New York, 1992, p. 108.

12   Botton began writing the book soon after leaving Roehampton and shelved it for almost twenty years. See Jane Dunn, *Antonia White: A Life*, London, 1998, pp. 45–47.

13   A favorable review of *Roman Spring* appeared in the *New York Times*, September 16, 1934.

14   For the offending passages, see Chanler, *Roman Spring*, pp. 184–86. Because of her Catholicism, Daisy was never welcomed at Rokeby by her sister-in-law Margaret Aldrich and none of her children or grandchildren was welcomed there later on.

15   Chanler, *Autumn in the Valley*, p. 58.

Bebo self portrait in oil 1934

CHAPTER 8

Years of Illness, 1936–37

BEBO'S PREDICTION IN HER OCTOBER 1935 LETTER TO Daisy was prescient for she was to spend the first half of 1936 and most of 1937 away from home, bedevilled with prolonged bouts of serious illness. In January 1936, suffering from rheumatism, sinus and "sweats", she wrote Daisy:

> I have changed doctors. Dr Boots was having a very bad effect on my nerves and as my nerves are much worse than my rheumatism, I decided to give a general practitioner a chance …[1] [Dr Neergaard] has cheered me up a lot and seems very intelligent about my hay-wire nerves. He thinks I have been in bed enough (Dr Boots gave me the jitters by telling me if I really wanted to get well, I should go to bed for a year and treat myself as though I had tuberculosis)!

She added that she was reading William James' *Varieties of Religious Experience* "for the first time" and was finding it a "really grand book."

Soon afterwards, following her doctor's orders, Bebo set out by train for Phoenix, Arizona, accompanied by a trained nurse, Miss Kurtz, whom Bebo called "a born traveller." They were stranded in New Orleans at night for a few hours between trains. Bebo and Miss Kurtz toured the city for an hour or so in a taxi and Bebo wrote Porter that she loved the city's nocturnal liveliness "after all those ratty southern towns I have been passing through."

For the next five months she underwent a period of rest and recuperation in a facility called the Desert Sanatorium in Tucson, Arizona, where she was diagnosed with rheumatic fever and pleurisy. According to a 1929 promotional pamphlet the sanatorium was a "non-profit 120-bed facility ... devoted to the treatment of the chronic diseases of bronchitis, asthma, emphysema, sinusitis, arthritis and polio. The desert's dry air and warm climate were believed to be beneficial to the treatment of these conditions."[2]

Bebo soon referred to the area as "this damn health zone" and the surrounding desert as "God forsaken" but by serendipity she discovered that the physician in charge of the sanatorium, a Dr Baldwin, had been raised in Rome and was the son of Daisy's family doctor in the 1880s.

In one of her first letters to Porter from Phoenix, Bebo wrote that she needed to be in bed for a month because

> I made such a hell of an effort to get here that I had a slight nervous collapse. They tell me my mind is much too active and that I mustn't talk read or think much. I shall become completely bovine and even less mentally alert than you are.

In a letter to Daisy in March, when she felt better, Bebo noted that

> This is a strange unearthly country not meant for human habitation but as it is also unsuitable for bacteria human beings flock here from all parts of the world to shed their bugs. Everything is consequently very artificial and uncozy ... Most

of the people in this court are deformed arthritics & I feel very spry & lucky in consequence. It all has the atmosphere of a convent with God left out.

At the sanatorium, Bebo drew a pleasing sketch, which I've inherited, of "the colored nurse's baby, black as the ace of spades but with a generic resemblance to all babies and therefore Mary."

By mid-March she was back to reading a good deal. After finishing George Santayana's autobiographical novel *The Last Puritan*, she wrote Porter that she had found it a "swell book and such a penetrating study of Priscilla [Auchincloss]'s soul."[3] To Daisy, she noted that the book was "an extraordinarily penetrating analysis of New England self-sufficiency and denseness. The hero hasn't the foggiest notion what truth is, yet he thinks he is dedicating his life to its pursuit."

One of the mysteries of Bebo's life from a twenty-first-century perspective is that such a curious, intellectually active woman could so happily succumb to the panoply and dogmatism of the Roman Catholic Church, which stood in her mind at the more pleasing end of a spectrum from what she called "self-sufficiency and denseness." Like her mother, Bebo was drawn to the rich intellectual and aesthetic traditions of the Church. She also believed in the divinity of Christ, transubstantiation, life after death and the efficacy of prayer. At another level, she preferred the security of the Church with its time-honored liturgy,[4] sacraments, papal decrees and so on to the idea that she or anyone else could manage or subdue life's problems (and perhaps especially the ones she faced) on their own. In his letter to me already quoted, Louis Auchincloss wrote:

> I did not share her passionate religious faith (your father told my mother that he believed her to be—literally—a saint) and it even struck me as a bit peculiar that so keen an intellect

could believe all the things she believed … but the union of such a brain with such a faith was very moving.[5]

In Phoenix as her health and morale appeared to improve, Bebo became cranky and impatient. On March 19 she wrote to Daisy: "For my temperature to stay down I have to be surrounded by desperately stupid people. They are plentiful here so I should improve!" and closed the letter: "Say a lot of prayers for me. I am leading a godless life here."

What she meant by "godless," I think, was that she was removed from the assurances, sacraments, rituals and social

Nurse's child: pencil sketch 1937

communion of the Church and was surrounded by people who saw their problems as physical and curable. All the same, as she wrote to Porter, "I daresay being depressed is better for me than all whoop-a-doops. I daresay being merry and bright takes up a lot of energy."

At the end of March an affectionate letter came from Dorothy Day, who reported that she and some of her colleagues, using the car that Porter had loaned them, had located a farm in Easton, Pennsylvania, that would be suitable for the Catholic Worker movement.[6] She added: "My sister was in a convalescent home last summer after her baby was born and she too spoke of the terrible self-absorption of the people around her." She closed by telling Bebo: "You are one of the sweetest of women and valiant in affection and I wish I could do something for you."

To keep her spirits up, Bebo asked Porter to send her a Latin dictionary and "some Nietzsche" and referred to herself as "an old pestiferous tree that suddenly feels the sap again." Her self-diagnosis was unduly optimistic. In early April Porter passed one of her letters along to Daisy in which Bebo had written:

> My poor dear mind has gone completely to pot since I began to feel so well. Maybe it was the bugs that made me so bright. There's certainly a big difference since the dear things left me … I'm much too stupid now to study Latin or anything else but I draw and draw all day long. I don't seem to be out of practice at all. I draw rather better in fact than when I left off a year ago last September. My day is as follows: walk for 1 hour from 6 to 7. Sunbathe 7 to 8, Breakfast on the patio then retires to hermetically sealed bedroom until 4:30 when heat becomes bearable again. Walk or drive before supper. Bed about 7:30.

Enclosing this letter, Porter commented:

Bebo's last letters have been fairly full of clinical details and are going the rounds of the medical profession in NY, to whom she continues to be a source of absorbing interest ... She doesn't seem to be making the progress that she had hoped, as far as the sinus is concerned; and the doctors don't seem to have gotten to the heart of the trouble, whereat I am much annoyed. Still the arthritis has improved & she been well enough to do a little drawing—apparently from a wheel chair.

In April, Bebo wrote to Porter *à propos* her gloomy surroundings: "Why are people so afraid of death? I can't imagine travelling three thousand miles to postpone death for a month or two perhaps."

In the following month she visited Santa Fe and the Grand Canyon with a couple named Rivington whom she had known in Washington in the 1920s. Mr Rivington had gone downhill in the meantime and Bebo wrote her mother that "he's clearly an alcoholic, looks like a beachcomber, bloodshot eyes, enormous paunch." As travelling companions Bebo found them

Both so elderly and unenthusiastic that they made me feel young and skittish and fascinating. I don't know how I'm going to face living with attractive & healthy people again.

The Grand Canyon, she wrote Porter, was "the only thing I ever want to see again" in the southwest. Some of her deft pencil sketches of the canyon have survived. One of Bebo's last letters from Phoenix asserted: "I'm holding onto myself with both hands so as not to be too whoops a daisy and get exhausted." In May she flew back to New York, an adventurous journey in those days. An early memory of mine is of going with Porter to a nearby airport, probably Newark, and running down a corridor to greet her. She was wearing a brown felt hat.

Bebo spent part of the summer recuperating at the Pickmans' summer place in Beverly, Massachusetts, writing to Porter:

> I am really on the mend now in a slow, steady, relaxed way. I don't feel like doing anything which is all to the good. Mummy says she knows now that whenever I say I'm fine I'm due for a relapse.

Toward the end of the year Bebo and Porter decided to board my brother Joe with a family in Massachusetts, close to Bebo's brother Teddy and his wife, who could look after him until Bebo had fully recovered. In fact, the arrangement whereby Joe lived mainly in Massachusetts, interrupted by sojourns in boarding schools, continued into the mid-1940s, with Joe making only occasional visits to us, especially to Geneseo. Unfortunately, none of the letters I have seen discusses the rationale for Joe's prolonged absences from the family and it's important to stress that for the rest of his life he enjoyed close, affectionate relations with both Bebo and Porter.

The next year, 1937, was probably the most distressing one in Bebo's life. The trouble began at Christmastime 1936 when she visited her sister Beatrice Allegaert, who had spent most of the year hospitalized in New York with a nervous breakdown. Bebo reported to Hester that Beatrice seemed "quite contented and very reasonable" except for the fact that "she insisted she & Pierre were not legally married." Beatrice was far from well and the specter of her continuing illness haunted Bebo during her own breakdown later in the year.

In January 1937, Bebo and Porter spent two weeks at a resort on Bermuda where she "painted a little for the first time in I don't know how long. Did one presentable landscape—the rest too fussy." With hindsight, the closing paragraph of the letter was ominous:

I got one of my attacks of general ailments on the boat but it passed kind of mild flu—so we have been a couple of crocks. Now all I ask now is that the sun should shine and I can sit blinking at it like an owl.

When she got back to New York she felt unwell and wrote Daisy on January 20:

Unfortunately, I'm on the blink again. Dr Boots wants me to go away again—for all of February anyway. He has limited me to 4 hours out of bed a day, which is not conducive to a hilarious life. I can't make up my mind about it. I *think* I'd rather stay home in bed than go wandering off. I'll decide in a few days.

Via special delivery Daisy, replied: "How sad the demon is still on the warpath! I am not altogether surprised but disappointed all the same. I so hoped he was going to give you peace."[7] Clearly more than rheumatism had been involved in Bebo's poor health in 1936, and what she called her "general ailments" covered a range of afflictions for which "the demon" seems as good a name as any.

In the 1930s, before the dominance in America of Freudian psychotherapy, "moral therapy" was the order of the day for most psychopathic patients.[8] For people like Bebo who could afford the cure, "rest" under controlled conditions whereby patients, closely monitored by therapists, could heal "naturally" was considered ideal and was usually what was prescribed.

With hindsight what ailed Bebo throughout her life as she often said later were not only her recurrent physical ailments, which ironically became largely "curable" for other people after she died, but also a long-term, depressive edginess and melancholia that may have been hereditary and were certainly exacerbated by the family pressures she increasingly came under in the 1930s.

These arose, I believe, from her being unexpectedly the mother of four children and from tensions that ricocheted against her from her childhood.

On January 31, 1937 in the words of a therapist, Bebo "woke up screaming and began walking in her sleep after a nightmare that her husband was crazy." For several days, the medical records continue, she "went through ceaseless self-analysis in which she related many happenings in her childhood." On February 9, she was driven in an ambulance with Porter and a nurse to a private psychiatric hospital, until 1936 known as Bloomingdale in White Plains, NY, a suburb of New York City, for treatment of what appeared to be a mental breakdown.[9]

Porter probably supplied her admission details. They generously listed her occupation as "painter" and limited her consumption of alcohol, which was not yet as problematic as it became later on, to "a social glass." In later life Bebo recalled her admission to the facility as a matter of relinquishing her engagement ring and then seeing nothing but spirals for perhaps a month. Her medical records, however, show that she was interviewed in detail on the day after she arrived.

Soon after Bebo was admitted Porter answered a letter from Bebo's aunt, Elizabeth Chapman, who had heard of Bebo's illness and had invited her to stay with her in Charleston, South Carolina, where she had a house. Porter replied that Bebo had just been admitted to Bloomingdale and Elizabeth answered on February 15:

> You have done wisely in taking Bebo to Bloomingdale, where everything is known about nervous and mental disturbances & where she will have absolute quiet. I have not given up hope of getting her down here for her convalescence. I could quite easily put up her nurse, and you too, into the bargain.[10]

When a psychiatrist interviewed her and asked, "Where

are we?" she answered, "I suspect Bloomingdale's, where most of us end up sooner or later." She was referring to her uncle Armstrong ("Archie") Chanler (1862–1934), who had been a patient in Bloomingdale for several years in the early 1900s before he escaped and fled to Virginia, where he changed his name to Chaloner and lived out his life in considerable style. In Virginia, estranged from his siblings, Archie supported local causes and was popular with local people, including African Americans, although he sometimes carried a silver-headed cane inscribed with the words "Leave me alone."[11] In the same interview, Bebo replied to a question about her "mental status":

> I thought I was off my balance a month ago or more. Told the doctor I thought so. He said I had to [straighten] it out by myself, work it out myself the best I could ... Felt it was the best I could do ... I thought I knew my courage was gone. Knew my physical strength was gone.

On the same day, Daisy wrote a four-page letter to Porter from Washington, DC, where she was spending the winter. She was replying to a telephone call that he had made to her on the previous evening to inform her of Bebo's hospitalization. Daisy thanked Porter for the call and apologized for not speaking to him herself (she had allowed her son Hubert who was with her at the time to take down the details) because she "would have wanted to ask too many questions." She added that she had had "a long letter from Teddy [about Bebo],[12] so your news did not go altogether unheralded." She continued:

> Laura told me that Dr Evans diagnosed Bebo's case as rather nervous-hysterical than mental—that she cannot sleep seems a most disquieting symptom—she who needs so much sleep—poor child ... I wish I could do something to lighten

her burdens. Troubles never come singly but always in pairs triplets or even quintuplets. I have great confidence in your power of dealing with them … One can only hope that the clouds will lift and the former equilibrium be restored.

After a few nights of insomnia and nightmares Bebo adjusted to the Bloomingdale regime and became a cooperative patient.[13] In late February her psychiatrist, Dr Burdick (who was, unusually for therapists in that era, a woman), noted that "she is interested in her illness, eager to understand the mechanisms and quite willing to remain for a period in the hospital, all of which speaks favorably for recovery from the psychotic phase." A few days later, Daisy unknowingly echoed Dr Burdick's view when she wrote to Porter that "[my] children tell me that [Bebo] quite likes being in the hospital and is in no hurry to come home."

Interestingly, a medical note about Bebo from mid-March 1937 stated, "She has been much interested in Buddhism. It is the self-discipline that interests her. She needs detached control." She never studied Buddhism in a systematic way, although she owned a copy of *Sur les traces du Bouddha* by René Grousset, which Daisy had sent to her from Paris in 1933.

In several revealing interviews with members of the staff, which survive in her medical records, Bebo provided scathing vignettes of her uncles and aunts, the Astor orphans, sparing only her aunt Elizabeth whom she called "a perfect saint" and her father, "a brilliantly witty man with a sunny disposition, more mercurial than his wife." On March 18, Dorothy Day wrote her:

As soon as it's permitted to have visitors, I want to come to see you. We all love you very much indeed … God must love you very much and think you strong enough to go through such trials, otherwise it would not happen. To me you are a very beautiful and lovely person and I have enjoyed being with you.

In another letter soon afterwards, Dorothy told Bebo that "you are one of those people that one is sure is all right and that God is taking care of." In a postcard to Porter at this time, Daisy wrote:

> Yesterday I got a nice letter from [Bebo] handwriting very steady—she sounds quite cheerful but never gives me her address and says you did not take her my letter. How can I reach her?

A month later, Daisy visited Bebo at Bloomingdale, an occasion that Bebo, writing Hester, found "exhausting" while taking care to write Daisy that "it was lovely to see you so well and serene."[14]

My sister Mary and I were too young to remember our mother's prolonged absences and of course we were unaware of their effect on Porter. I found out after he died, when I inherited his stamp collection, that a great deal of the collection had been assembled and fastidiously catalogued in 1936 and 1937 when Bebo was in Phoenix and White Plains and when Porter had no idea that she would re-emerge in good health. He never mentioned the intense loneliness and uncertainty that he must have suffered in these years. No letters exchanged between Porter ad Bebo while she was in the hospital have survived.

I do remember that each night when Porter came to tuck me in during the English Coronation Year of 1937, taking Bebo's place, he told me a story about every English king and queen from William the Conqueror to George VI, using a poster with cameo portraits of the kings that he'd pinned onto my bedroom wall. He had something interesting to say about each of the monarchs. At other times, he could perform the same task with American presidents. The ebb and flow of narrative history, especially of England and the United States, was a sustaining interest of Porter's throughout his life.

Over the summer as Bebo's condition gradually improved Porter made arrangements for Judie to board temporarily with a family named Lee in Concord, Massachusetts, near the Pickmans, while she attended school nearby. Judie spent the summer at Westerly before these arrangements took effect.

In July 1937, sensing that Bebo was getting better, Hester wrote to her supportively:

> There's nothing like a good breakdown to make over the Chanler girls! There's something in our engines that tends to skip but which can quite as well run correctly. I'm sure you'll always be stronger as a result of these dreary months.

In her reply, Bebo returned to a familiar topic, their mother, writing about Daisy's

> Horror of being bored—of that strange gray look that comes into her face—it is like a fog that chills the marrow and sometimes I gather more people around than we can stand to ward it off.

Bebo's health improved steadily over the summer, when she wrote good-natured letters to Daisy and Hester. On Daisy's seventy-fifth birthday in August, she wrote that she had received "a long analytical letter from Teddy. He writes seldom but when he does it is really worth while." The letter unfortunately hasn't survived. Later in the month, after she had been told she could spend a week in Westerly, she wrote Daisy that she was finding Gerard Manley Hopkins' *Notebooks* "slow going" and that she was "bogged" in Pick's recently published book, *The Mind of Latin Christendom.*[15]

> and it couldn't keep my interest. Heresies are so boring and he writes about them in just the same spirit as he quotes St

Augustine. If you have no nose for absolute truth how deadly life must be.

Of course, Bebo knew perfectly well that her brother-in-law's life wasn't "deadly" and that her long friendship with him would survive her judgment of his book. She probably meant that if she ever became unmoored from what she took to be absolute truth embodied in her religion she would be in danger of becoming spiritually dead.

The doctors at Bloomingdale decided that Bebo's condition had improved to the extent that she could be provisionally released in March 1938 after extended visits to Geneseo and New York City. In April she visited Joe and Judie in Massachusetts and finalized arrangements for their schooling in the fall. She was formally discharged from the hospital in October 1938, but the box "cured" on her release paper was not ticked. As we will see, Bebo returned to the hospital with similar but damaging symptoms in February 1953.

Notes

1   Dr Neergaard, a genteel Yale graduate, was the family doctor for many years. He signed Bebo's death certificate in 1958.

2   (No author), *The Desert Sanatorium and Institute of Research*. Phoenix, AZ, 1929. Fees per month at the sanatorium were $452.75, close to $5000 in today's dollars, a figure that ironically recalls the monthly wages paid to Daisy's staff at Sweetbriar.

3   Ironically, Priscilla wrote Bebo in Phoenix that she hadn't enjoyed the book.

4   In a letter to Hester in 1939 Bebo calls the liturgy "the life-blood of the church circulating over the globe."

5   Louis Auchincloss, letter of August 6, 2000.

6   See Andrew Sheehan, *Peter Maurin: Gay Believer*. New York, 1959, p. 104. In the 1950s, of course, the word "gay" did not yet have its present connotation. In June 1936 Porter drove Dorothy to the farm, and during the trip gave her "a lot of free legal advice."

7   In May 1936, writing to Bebo about Beatrice, Daisy had used the phrase "old dragons" to describe Beatrice's nervous breakdown. In her letter to Bebo, she added: "I know how you hate to go into the wilderness in search of health."

8   Lloyd Sederer, "Moral Therapy and the Problem of Morale", *American Journal of Psychiatry*, vol. 134, no. 3 (March 1977), pp. 267–72. See also J. Sanbourne Bockhoven, MD, "Moral Treatment in American Psychiatry", *Journal of Nervous and Mental Disease*, vol. 124 (1956), pp. 167–94 and 292–321. I'm grateful to Dr Steven Roth for sending me copies of these insightful papers.

9   See William Logie Russell, *The New York Hospital: A History of the Psychiatric Service*. New York, 1945. Dr Steven Roth is writing a history of the hospital, covering the years since Russell's book appeared.

10   Elizabeth died later in 1937. In 1925, Hester had convalesced in Charleston at her home.

11   See Donna M. Lucey, *Archie and Amelie: Love and Madness in the Gilded Age*. New York, 2006; and John Armstrong Chaloner, *Four Years behind the Bars at Bloomingdale*. Roanoke, 1906, a robust, unhinged account of what he believed had been his illegal incarceration.

12   Teddy's letter to Daisy has not survived, nor have all but one of the letters that Porter and Bebo exchanged while she was a patient at Bloomingdale.

13   Interestingly, a medical note about Bebo from mid-March 1937 stated, "She has been much interested in Buddhism. It is the self-discipline that interests her. She needs detached control." She never studied Buddhism in a systematic way, although she owned a copy of *Sur les traces du Bouddha* by René Grousset, sent to her by Daisy from Paris in 1933.

14   In the only letter from Porter to Bebo in Bloomingdale that seems to have survived he wrote: "I was sorry you had been so tired by your mother's visit. It is inevitable, I think, that she should be a bit unaware of things—it's a sort of protective armor she has developed."

15   Edward Motley Pickman, *The Mind of Latin Christendom*. Oxford, 1937.

CHAPTER 9

The Pre-war Years, 1938–41

THROUGH ALL THE FAMILY PROBLEMS THAT ASSAILED him in these years, Porter's career as a corporate lawyer advanced rapidly and he became a partner in Davis Polk at about the time Bebo was released from Bloomingdale.

Over the next three years, Bebo resumed work on her painting. Her letters from the period reflect her renewed concerns about her children and problems connected with moving Daisy from Sweetbriar to Massachusetts once her mobility became impaired. Throughout the period there were shadows cast by the imminence of the war in Europe that broke out in September 1939.

I can hardly remember Bebo's absence in 1936–37 but afterwards, when my memories of her begin to "kick in", they are entirely favorable. Our times together in New York at least were limited to the governess's day off and to sessions at the end of the day when she often read aloud to Mary and me from her own childhood favorites — *The Princess and the Goblins* by George MacDonald, *The Amulet* by E. Nesbit and the colored fairy books assembled by Andrew Lang.

In these years Bebo painted several watercolors in a *faux-naïf* style, usually on religious themes. They have a jewel-like luminousness of color and a pleasing, almost stained-glass quality. She wrote about one of them in a letter to Daisy:

> I showed you the Holy Innocents when you were here; it's a framed water-color of 12 children dancing around with palms. Some of the children [have] a vague resemblance to David and Mary but it was not intentional.

In the late 1930s and for the rest of her life Bebo relished the movies she went to see, especially French ones from this period such as *Pepé le Moko*, *Le Jour se Lève* and *Quai des Brumes*. After seeing George Cukor's film of Claire Booth's play *The Women* in 1939, she wrote Daisy that it "included every obnoxious female type except the Chanler girls."

One afternoon in the summer of 1938 I vividly recall looking through Porter's binoculars I found that I could distinguish the edges of leaves on the trees. I had probably been very nearsighted since birth. It's unnerving to think that I was five and a half before anybody noticed. When we returned to the city, I was fitted with glasses at Lugene's at 81st Street and Madison, and started at the Buckley School for Boys on East 74th Street. I stayed at the school until the spring of 1943, shepherded there by governesses who also picked me up in the afternoon except on their days off when Bebo took their place.

Medical emergencies continued to dog the family. In the winter of 1939, I was operated on in New York for an infected mastoid.[1] The infection reappeared in August and I was operated on again, this time in Rochester, followed almost immediately by an emergency removal of my appendix.

At some point in that year, Porter used a yellow legal pad to itemize the family's medical expenses over the past decade—in other words, since he had started working at Davis Polk:

1929: $1755
1930: $1506
1931: $810
1932: $1035
1933: $2860
1934: $891
1935: $2945
1936: $3432
1937: $4996
1938: $537
1939: $3931

The total of $24,698 is equivalent in today's dollars to $286,522, a sizeable slice of Porter's substantial income.[2] The "spikes" in 1933 and 1935 reflected the costs of births in private hospitals while those of 1936 and 1937 reflected the costs of Bebo's hospitalizations. The spike in 1939 was due to my own bouts of hospitalization.

Another problem, for Bebo at least, arose in the spring of 1939 when Daisy's legs gave out at Sweetbriar and she had to be driven across the lawn to attend Mass at St Felicity's. Bebo asked Hester to send a wheelchair from Bedford, which duly arrived, but Daisy's future at Sweetbriar, a large three-story house, had become a dubious proposition. Two years earlier Bebo's brother Hubert, a career naval officer, had married Gertrude Laughlin in Washington, DC. It was understood that he would inherit Sweetbriar, a process that was accelerated by the prospect of Daisy's moving out.[3]

On July 8, 1939, for their fifteenth wedding anniversary, Porter gave Bebo a silver brooch embedded with several small sapphires. On the inside of the brooch he had a Latin epigram that read as follows: 'Nec ferat ulla dies ut commutemur in aevo quin tibi sim iuvenis tuque puella mihi.' (And let no day come when we be changed in age, but that I should be your boy and you my girl.)[4]

That same summer, Father Andrew Rogosh of the Russian Roman Catholic rite, whom Bebo had met through Dorothy Day, visited us in Geneseo. He was charming, but he was also a strain, as Bebo wrote Hester:

> He got one of those graft drivers' licenses after 5 lessons and insists on driving all the time & he's perfectly awful and gives me the willys. He has so much fun doing it though that I can't forbid him to drive.

Father Rogosh was a delightful, bearded man whom I remember well. Trained in Rome, he'd arrived in the United States in 1935. He remained a friend of Bebo's for the rest of her life and was one of the priests who officiated at her memorial service in November 1958. During his first visit to Geneseo, Father Rogosh said Russian rite Masses in St Felicity's, while Daisy was away in Massachusetts, spending a few weeks by the sea. Bebo wrote to her:

> We are having a beautiful time at the chapel every morning—Gertrude [Hubert's 23-year-old wife] and I are making the long responses in English, as our old Slavonic is not too hot and the short Slavonic responses in Slavonic with a Hungarian accent. Our books are printed phonetically for Hungarians.[5]

Later that summer Bebo accompanied my brother Joe to the Sunlight Ranch in Cody, Wyoming, for a vacation that they both enjoyed until it was cut short by my medical emergency. She wrote Porter that the ranch with its communal life and set routines "approximates [the hospital] Bloomingdale's without the undesirable features—e.g. the nuts and the ideology", adding that she had been reproved for taking a flask of whiskey on a ranch-sponsored hayride.

Bebo came east to visit me in the hospital in Rochester. That must have been in early September, because I remember being shown photographs in the hospital depicting the first days of the war in Europe. I returned to Buckley at some point in the fall. For most of 1940, as part of my convalescence, I was kept away from strenuous exercise and spent many afternoons in bed.

Bebo stayed briefly with Hester in late 1939 and wrote her afterwards from Geneseo:

> I left my white woolen sock I was knitting for Porter with a long green one of his wrapped up in a Chinese handkerchief I think in the living room. I also borrowed the letters of St Francis Xavier.

In 1939 Joe began visiting a psychiatrist named Marion Putnam in Boston on a weekly basis, presumably for help in managing the impulsive, risk-taking behavior that was getting him into trouble at school.

Meanwhile, in New York, a wry Glaswegienne named Catherine Gillies took over as the governess for Mary, Judie and me. Catherine was tough-minded, affectionate and fun to be with. I remember that when we asked her if we *had* to do something or other that she had asked us to do, her curt and memorable reply was "Die". Catherine stayed with us until June 1943, shortly before Porter returned from overseas. She told Bebo at that point that she was unwilling to spend the summer at Westerly if there were no permanent servants. A replacement named Miss Brooks proved to be a disaster and left soon afterwards. Mary and I had no governesses after that.

At some point in 1940—I remember the cold weather—Bebo

took me to visit Laura and her family on Long Island and wrote to Daisy:

> Annie [the youngest White] tried to snub [David] with old world sophistication but he never seemed to realize that he was being snubbed and went on being exceedingly amiable so after a while she gave it up and they became fast friends. They were terribly cunning together.

In 1940 Great Britain was at war with Germany while America was not. As the German bombing of British cities intensified, Bebo and Porter's English friends Roger and Constance Stevens, living in London, proposed sending their son Bryan, who was a year younger than me and also Porter's godson, to stay with us for the duration of the war.[6] Bebo and Porter agreed and Bryan was due to arrive in July after Porter had left for officer training camp in Plattsburg, NY. Bebo wrote a comically agitated letter to him at this point:

> I sent off a whole bunch of telephone electricity Kammin [dry cleaners] etc to Miss Collins [Porter's secretary?] to pay and I got a letter telling me she was on vacation. A very neat trick I must say Mr Chandler, to try and get me to pay those bills and I *won't*. Not a cent did I get for taking Joe to camp—I'm off tomorrow to get Bryan and what am I to use for money, Mr Chandler, buttons, I suppose.

She added that she was

> Just back from 24 hours with [her friends] the Cunninghams in Rochester—saw lots of intelligent people and talked my head off. Drank too much and had a high old time generally.

A few days later Bebo wrote to Daisy:

The English boy arrived last week and is a perfect darling. No trouble at all and very good fun to have around. Beautifully brought up. I hope my children catch his manners.

Unfortunately, despite Bebo's kindness and optimism, Bryan had terrible nightmares and Mary and I made his stay unpleasant. I was jealous of the handful of English toys that he brought with him. Mary and I teased him unmercifully, despite being scolded for our behavior by Catherine Gillies. Bebo wrote Porter that "we are having plenty of hard moments with Bryan but he's really a lovely child." After a month or so at Westerly, arrangements were made for him to spend the remainder of the war in Cooperstown, New York, with other friends of his parents.[7]

In that same summer Bebo took on the daunting task of clearing Daisy's clothes and possessions out of Sweetbriar, pending her mother's move to Massachusetts. On July 24, she wrote Daisy:

> Do you want Minnie Servis [the wife of the groom at Sweetbriar] to wipe off all the leather-bound books in the library & the drawing room? She says it would be about three days' work and I really think it's necessary.

The same letter described mountains of clothes, handbags, dressing gowns ("there are ever so many dressing gowns—Japanese and Chinese house-coats") and closed with: "PS There are dozens of white suede shoes. Do you want any of them or shall give them to the rummage sale?"

Back in New York that fall Bebo resumed a calmer, more literary correspondence with her mother. She had been reading Etienne Gilson's *Reason and Revelation in the Middle Ages* "and enjoyed it very much but it is *une oeuvre de haute vulgarisation* (I came across the term the other day and love the idea of high vulgarity)." In December she was immersed once again in the writings of the French Catholic writer Léon Bloy:[8]

> I have been reading Bloy almost steadily for the last 24 hours
> ever since Joan Cunningham took me to hear [Jacques]
> Maritain's lecture about him. I have always shied off Bloy, as
> I understood he was "strong meat" and I'm rather sick of being
> turned upside down—but it's really great stuff if you can stand
> it. I said a few words to Maritain afterwards and thought he
> was a lovely man—a really wonderful look in his eye!

At about this time Bebo became president of the Women's Unit for War Relief, a New York–based Catholic charitable organization. She wrote her mother that she was unhappy with the appointment but was unable to back down even though the job would involve "endless meetings and hullabaloo." Cuttings from the *New York Times* indicate that she remained on the committee for at least ten years. In early 1941, she wrote Daisy:

> I went to tea at Germane Wilson's today and met a group of
> very distinguished and completely penniless French refugees.
> I felt more "mink coat" than ever (fortunately I don't own a
> mink coat!) but Davis Polk seems hopelessly over-stuffed
> just now and there's no use pretending I'm not one of the
> over-privileged.

Bebo visited Boston in May 1941 and stayed with Hester. As part of her ongoing concern about Joe, she talked with Dr Putnam, Joe's psychologist, but she left an unfortunate impression, as Dr Putman wrote to Porter:

> I hope I did not over fatigue Mrs Chandler. She looked
> suddenly very tired in the last few minutes. The subject of
> Joe is always agitating when we meet so seldom and I'm

sometimes left with the fear that Mrs Chandler feels I am blaming her for Joe's difficulties. I am not.

I think her feeling that Joe's problems, which turned out to be transitory, might be permanent, may have agitated Bebo but she and Joe maintained a close, confiding relationship for the rest of her life.

During her visit to Boston Bebo suffered from recurrent health problems. She needed to have her ears drained and was under some strong, unspecified medication. She had a nurse when she stayed with Hester and amid what she called the "Pickman hullabaloo" she forgot Porter's birthday and wrote to apologize to him. She closed the letter by telling him:

> Everything I complain of is put down to the [unspecified] drug. The doctor says I should be very bad tempered—that the drug always makes people ugly. That hasn't come yet but maybe will just as I get back to NY.

That summer, Porter became a Roman Catholic. None of the letters I have seen discusses the run-up to this momentous event but I don't remember being taken by surprise. After all, Porter had always been a devout, church-going Episcopalian. Years later he told me that he had made the choice partly by drawing up a list of pros and cons (probably on one of his yellow legal pads) and found the pros convincing. Pressure from Bebo over the years had been light but insistent, as when she pointed out in the 1930s that after an unlikely series of deaths Princess Margaret Rose, not yet a teenager, could became the titular head of the Anglican Church. More importantly, Porter's study of the life and behavior of Henry VIII and his entourage made him unhappy with the historical foundations of English Protestantism.

Predictably, however, he became an English-oriented

Catholic much as Daisy had become a Roman-oriented one. When he was confirmed, Bebo wrote to Daisy that he had taken as his saint's name "Thomas for St Thomas More who had more to do with his conversion than anyone else." Porter was pleased to choose an English lawyer as his patron saint. A framed reproduction of Hans Holbein's portrait of More hung in his New York bedroom for the remainder of his life. Porter never spoke of the spiritual rationale for his conversion but his Catholic faith was a great source of assurance and spiritual nourishment for him especially in the years after Bebo's death.

Over the summer of 1941 the last of Daisy's possessions, including a Rubens drawing, were transported from Sweetbriar to Bedford, Massachusetts, where she lived for more than a decade in a house near Hester's in what was until the 1970s a kind of Pickman family compound that I visited often from the mid 1950s onward. When the move had been accomplished, Bebo wrote Hester: "Now that the last nail has been driven in the last packing case, I can dismiss the whole painful business."

Notes

1   Mastoiditis is an inflammation in the mastoid bone immediately behind the ear. The disease is caused by an infection and often required surgery in the years before World War II. It's curable nowadays with sulfa drugs.

2   Nicholas Clifford (email, May 5, 2012) sensibly wondered if the family had health insurance. I doubt it, as these figures seem to represent payouts rather than bills taken care of at least in part by insurers.

3   In July 1940, Bebo wrote Hester that "Hubert's adoration of [Sweetbriar] is really quite comic. I don't believe the Sackville Wests take Knole any more seriously."

4   My daughter Maggie inherited the brooch, copied the inscription and sought out a translation. Judith Herrin gave this one to me in 2017. The epigram was by the Roman poet and administrator Ausanios (310–396 AD), a native of what is now Bordeaux.

5   Father Rogosh took charge of St Michael's Russian rite church on Mulberry Street in lower Manhattan, near the offices of the *Catholic Worker*. He died in 1969.

6   Roger Stevens (1906–1980) retired from the diplomatic service with a knighthood in the late 1960s after having served as ambassador to Sweden and Iran. He was later chancellor of the University of Leeds. Susan and I met Roger and his wife and Bryan in 1971 when we visited Britain with Porter.

7   The family was reunited in 1943 when Roger Stevens became British consul-general for the Rocky Mountain States. Susan and I met Bryan in London in 1971, when he gave us some sound advice about Australia.

8   When she encountered Bloy's work in 1939, Bebo urged Hester and Daisy to read it, noting in one letter that Bloy "produces intellectual indigestion if read in too large doses."

CHAPTER 10

The Chandlers and the War

I REMEMBER HEARING ABOUT THE JAPANESE ATTACK ON PEARL Harbor on the radio as I had supper in bed (my regime in 1940–41, as I recovered from hospitalizations).[1] Porter's reaction to America's declaration of war was to volunteer for service almost at once and early in 1942 he was commissioned as a captain in the Army Air Corps. His patriotism was sincere and deeply felt but at forty-two he was ineligible for the draft and very few of his colleagues at Davis Polk took up the call to service as quickly or as eagerly as he did. What's more, the difficulties that his going off to war might cause Bebo and his family don't seem to have entered his calculations at the time.

The war years formed an important watershed for the Chandlers as they did for countless millions of other people. None of us suffered in a serious way but our lifestyle, medicines and labor-saving devices, to name only three, became very different after 1945. Vacuum cleaners, dishwashers, washing machines and dryers, air-travel and frozen food all appeared in our lives after the war and after 1946 my parents no longer employed any live-in servants. As far as medications are concerned, by 1946 Bebo's ear problems could have been easily treated by sulfa drugs that had been unavailable before the war.

The war was more of an ordeal for Bebo than it was for Porter. Family income fell sharply although Davis Polk paid its absent partners a percentage of what they might have earned. For the first time in her life Bebo had to manage the household and the farm in Geneseo on her own. She was also thrown among her restive children all day long for the first time in her life. When she was readmitted to Bloomingdale with a nervous collapse in 1953, she recalled that after Porter had gone overseas in 1942 she was faced with a domestic help problem, had her two younger children at home and both were inclined to be wild. She began to drink heavily at about this time, was anxious and tense most of the time.

Bebo was a patriotic citizen but she often said later that at Porter's age and with his analytical skills he might well have found more appropriate military work closer to home—as he was to do in Army Intelligence in Washington from 1943 to 1945. His rush to combat, which was "in character" given his deep sense of duty, is still hard for me to understand.

Bebo wrote Daisy in early 1942 that Porter had angled for an assignment to an air base in England "which is his heart's desire, but fills me with misgivings, but there's nothing I can do about it." I doubt that Porter absorbed her misgivings, and in any case by July 1942 was an intelligence officer with the 66th US fighter squadron attached with several other American fighter squadrons to the British 8th Army. The 66th took part in the battle of El Alamein and Porter stayed with it until the capture of Tunis in June 1943—a year-long separation from Bebo and his family. He returned home as a major with two battle stars and a Distinguished Unit Citation. Porter was always immensely proud of his war experiences and they take up a large portion of his contribution to the 50th anniversary class report to Harvard College, which he wrote in 1971.[2]

In the spring, Bebo arranged to move with Mary and me to a smaller, less expensive apartment at 108 East 82nd Street, taking up the lease in September when we got back from Geneseo. Before she left 320, she wrote Daisy that "I feel quite sad about breaking up the [old] apartment—10 years is a big chunk of one's life."

In August, still without recent news from Porter, she attended Daisy's eightieth birthday celebrations in Bedford, a gala family occasion that Bebo referred to in a letter to Daisy later on as a "lovely apotheosis." In the same letter, written from Westerly, she added that she was "running the place with two maids and just one man which means everything is only half done, but it's still way beyond my means." She was also managing the farm—a daunting task, as she wrote to Daisy:

> I find myself very stupid at it all but I daresay I shall get
> brighter in time, it's a question of putting one's whole mind
> on very tiresome details and never dropping a stitch, as there
> always seems to be someone on the spot to pick up the stitch
> if it is to his own advantage!

Porter, meanwhile, was on the move in the Egyptian and then the Libyan desert, conscientiously performing his duties and cheerfully enduring harsh weather, erratic supplies and occasional danger. The campaign was a fast-moving, victorious advance through an almost uninhabited landscape and fighting alongside British and Commonwealth forces pleased Porter's Anglophilic turn of mind. His morale never faltered and his cheerful, perceptive letters from North Africa, which he assembled into a typewritten volume in 1974, were always a joy for us to read. They told of shortages of potable water, scorpions, bats, sandstorms, Roman ruins and playing games of Monopoly with the other officers in the squadron. He seldom mentioned the dangers he was encountering from German air raids and he never wrote about the deaths in combat of several of the squadron's pilots.

He returned home in June 1943 and Bebo wrote Daisy from Washington where Porter was being debriefed and where she went to meet him that "he is in wonderful shape—looks very young and handsome." A few days later, Porter went on leave to Westerly and Bebo wrote to her mother:

> Life has been very hectic since Porter got home, as his one idea is that everything should be as comfortable as ever! Hubert [just back from a year in the Pacific] is the same. The fact that they have been without servants of any kind for so long makes them feel any kind of maid should produce all kinds of luxury! My cook left in a pet after he had been here two days! I now have a nice little high school girl who doesn't know much and the mother of my beloved Whitneys, who is old and feeble but very willing. We are getting along all right but I am kept on the run all day, as nobody knows anything.

In another letter to Daisy at this time she wrote:

> This place always seems nonsensical without [Porter] and when he's home it mysteriously becomes dignum et justum—I suppose it is because he loves it so, and radiates satisfaction.

Soon afterwards Porter was posted to the Air Intelligence School in Harrisburg, Pennsylvania. Bebo visited him there and wrote a long letter about the place to Daisy, noting that Porter "seems ever so much better than he was in Geneseo and is definitely himself again ... He has no idea where he will be sent; but if it's in any way possible I shall join him with David and Mary." The rest of the letter benefits from the fact that it was written on a large piece of paper rather than the small, letterhead stationery

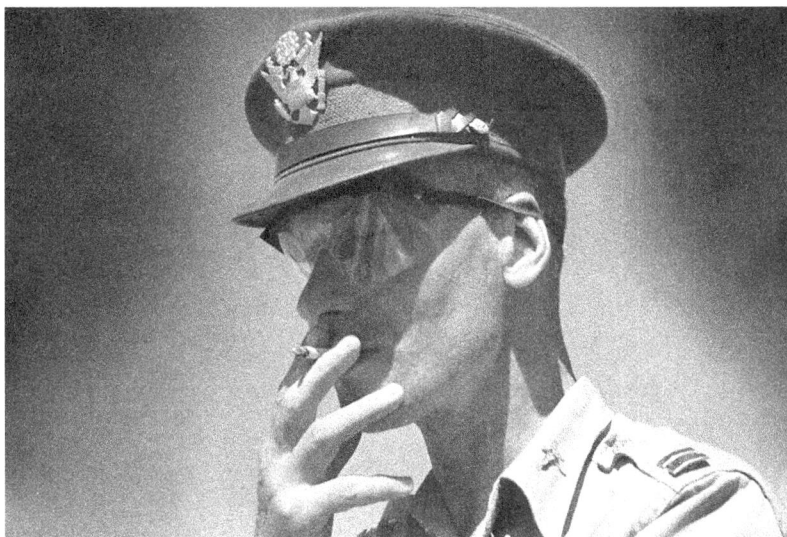

Porter's war: Libya winter 1943

that she normally used. Reading it I can overhear her voice.

The letter describes a visit to Hershey, Pennsylvania, a town near Harrisburg where America's most popular chocolates, also called Hershey, were manufactured in enormous quantities:[3]

> We went on one expedition to Hershey where all the chocolate is made. It is a fantastic place—completely Brave New World. Everything—drug stores, hospital, hotel etc belongs to Mr Hershey who is 85 and completely uneducated. He wants his workers to be happy so he lavishes money on anything thinks they would like—a zoo, a Coney Island amusement park, the largest ice-skating rink in the world, outdoor and indoor theatres. He has the best musical comedies come from NY and the best dance orchestras but not a speck of culture to be found anywhere: I think it would be your hell! The streets are called West Chocolate Avenue and Cocoa Boulevard etc. The architecture is awful and the people love it. They are born

here and die under his paternalistic regime ... I must now take my daily trip to the State liquor store. Liquor is very scarce & most days they haven't got anything fit to drink but by going every day one manages to acquire a couple of bottles a week!

In October 1943 Porter transferred from the Air Corps to the US Army General Staff and was posted to the recently completed Pentagon building south of Washington, DC, the home of what was then called the War Department. Until the end of the war he worked hard and happily in the Intelligence Division alongside many old friends from New York law firms who had chosen less dramatic military careers.

The family followed him to Washington, DC, where we rented a three-story Victorian house at 3405 N Street in Georgetown, a part of the city that had yet to take on the gloss that it acquired later. Georgetown was filled at the time with handsome early nineteenth-century houses and tumbledown cottages that were later restored or torn down. Harry Hopkins, President Roosevelt's *éminence grise*, lived on the opposite corner, while facing us on N Street was a dilapidated single-story house with a dirt floor, a bedraggled family named Corbin and, as I recall, no electricity.

We arrived in Washington after the schools had opened and it was difficult at first to place Mary and me in private schools. I was finally enrolled in Georgetown Preparatory School in suburban Maryland, while a slot was found for Mary at the Sacred Heart convent school on Dupont Circle. I'd skipped from Grade 5 to Grade 7 to get into Georgetown and was at least a year younger than any of my classmates. The school seemed rough after the gentility of Buckley and for the first year I was nervous and unhappy and made few friends.

For Bebo running the household in Washington was a continual strain. Although she could shop, embroider, knit, darn socks, paint and sculpt, she had never done laundry, ironed a shirt or cleaned a house. She cooked very few meals except for her own pleasure before she was forty-six. She employed a series of cooks in Washington but she was often saddled with most of the housekeeping chores. She told psychiatrists in the 1950s that she drank "pretty heavily" in those years.

Soon after we arrived, she learned that her nephew Peter White was planning to marry Jehanne Price, whom Bebo had befriended before the war when Jehanne was a student at Manhattanville College. The wedding in November 1943 was in a Georgetown church because Peter, an Army captain, was at that stage working in the Pentagon. The reception was held in our N St house. Mary and I had a noisy fight in the church and were removed as the wedding was going on.[4] At the reception, our squabbling continued and we had to be separated from the guests. At the ages of ten and eight, it seems, we were as nervy and "impossible" as Bebo had been at the same stage of her life.

Bebo's years in Washington were also rewarding and involved a kind of opening out. She embarked on a lifelong friendship with the warm-hearted, eccentric English author Anne Fremantle,[5] and on another with a lively sociologist at Catholic University named Dorothea Sullivan. She and Porter were also members of the Washington, DC, branch of the Catholic Interracial Council, which had been founded in 1934 by John LaFarge S.J. (1880–1963), a friend of Bebo and Porter's, and since the 1920s a crusader for African-American civil rights. The branches strove to improve the treatment of African-American Catholics in Washington, then a Southern city in which the Church treated African Americans as second-class citizens.[6] As a matter of course African Americans in Washington received communion separately from whites.

Working on the council meant that Bebo was interacting

socially with African Americans for the first time. In 1945 she wrote to Hester: "I'm off in a few minutes to an all-day interracial day of recollection, men and women, black and white, first time in history down here."

She and Porter also renewed their friendship with the British diplomat "Jock" Balfour, then working in the British Embassy, as he had been when they had met him in 1924.[7] Gertrude Chanler's widowed mother, Thérèse Laughlin, lived in the splendid 16th Street mansion that her diplomat husband had had built between the wars and Porter's cousin, Congressman James Wadsworth, lived a few blocks away from us in a handsome house on P Street.

In the summer of 1944 Mary went off to summer camp and Bebo and I travelled to Woods Hole and Martha's Vineyard, Massachusetts, where we stayed for a few days with Hester, Pick and Daisy in a rented cottage.[8] I spent much of the time composing an illustrated 70-page novel about interwar skulduggery called 'Travels of an Outcast'. It was filled with ambushes, escapes and villains identifiable by scars and poorly waxed moustaches. In August the journal *Modern Music* printed a cartoon of Bebo's depicting her brother Teddy. She drew the cartoon to accompany an article about his celebrated songs.[9]

When we got back to Washington in the fall I fitted in more easily at Georgetown and Bebo fell into a more congenial rhythm of housekeeping and social life. As she wrote to Daisy:

> Even though life is complicated down here it is so much easier the second year when you know all the ropes. I look upon this time last year as the all time low. Now that I'm more efficient it isn't all that bad.

There were still problems in the family, of course. Porter worked long hours and played a limited role in raising Mary and me. At one stage he told Bebo that an opportunity had arisen for him to go on a protracted mission to China. I'm glad I wasn't in the room to overhear her reaction. The opportunity sank without a trace.[10]

In March 1945 Bebo wrote a letter to the *Washington Post* objecting to the documentary film *Fury in the Pacific* that showed what she called a "scared 'Rochester' type" as the only African American. Rochester was the name of the radio comedian Jack Benny's feckless African-American servant who was the butt of Benny's humor. The clip had drawn a laugh from the audience and this made Bebo "ashamed of my race. If I were the mother of a colored soldier, I would feel it was the last straw." Her letter was reprinted in the *Afro American* ten days later. Over Easter, Bebo was hit with one of her perennial staffing crises and wrote to Daisy:

> I finally got a maid after 3 weeks without one, during which time I got so cross and tired that life was almost unbearable! I don't know why it should be so difficult when 99 1/2% of the human race do their own work and at least 80% without the benefit of electricity! But there it is.

For my part, I remember the spring of 1945 with pleasure. I'd made some friends by then and had decent marks at school. I knew my way around Washington by bus and trolley. I haunted the R Street library in Georgetown and collected stamps, pennies and hundreds of bottle caps, which I arranged into military formations in the cellar of our house. On weekends, I careened around the city, went to movies and took frightening rides at the Glen Echo Amusement Park, usually with a friend from school, a thirteen-year-old French count known in those days as Sanche de Gramont.[11]

My parents and Joe had agreed that Joe should join the Navy

when he turned seventeen in July. He enlisted just before the end of the war and emerged two years later a changed young man, eager to complete his high school education under the GI Bill.

Porter was discharged from the Army as a lieutenant colonel in August 1945. When he took leave in Geneseo that summer Bebo painted his portrait in uniform at his request. She also painted a portrait of me that my son Tom refers to as "a Hitler Youth" because of my side-brushed blond hair and dim-sighted light-blue eyes. She painted another of her niece Cynthia White (later Jay), who was visiting us that summer. Cynthia told me recently that Mary and I were both "horrible" at the time.

Bebo's burst of creative energy flowed into 1946 in New York, when she did a portrait of a friend's child and a couple of effective still lifes but after that her painterly output tapered off.

Notes

1   Hubert and his family were stationed in Honolulu but during the attack Hubert was at sea. On December 8, Bebo wrote Daisy: "Poor Gertrude! I suppose we won't hear for some time how they are."

2   In our extended family, Bebo's brother Hubert earned a Silver Star for bravery in the Battle of the Coral Sea and her sister Beatrice's elder son, Francis Allegaert, was killed in September 1944 as an infantryman near Nancy, France. He was 20. In 2014, his brother Winthrop ("Win") Allegaert compiled an history of Francis's unit in the Battle of France.

3   The letters that she wrote on 9 x 11 inch paper from Cleveland, Phoenix and Bloomingdale are among her best "partly because there was more paper to write on."

4   When we met in May 2010, Jehanne fondly recalled our unruliness at her wedding and told me that Bebo was "a truly free spirit" who had remembered her and Peter in her will "at a time when we really needed the money." Jehanne died in January 2013.

5   Bebo was godmother to Anne's youngest son, Hugh, born (like Susan) in August 1944. Hugh and I renewed our acquaintance in 2007.

6   For a positive reference to Bebo's work, see *Indianapolis Recorder*, an African-American newspaper, 6 January 1945.

7   Sir John Balfour (1894-1983) was later ambassador to Argentina and Spain. We caught up with him in London in 1971. His autobiography, *Not too Correct an Aureole: Recollections of a Diplomat*, appeared in 1983.

8   At the cottage we learned of the Allied invasion of southern France, which occurred in the week Susan was born. In the 1950s Bebo, referring to my unknown wife-to-be, used to say to me that "the poor thing is out there some-where"—as indeed she was.

9   Robert Tangman, "The Songs of Theodore Chanler." *Modern Music* 22 (May–June 1945), pp. 227–33. See also Victoria Ethier Villamil, *A Singer's Guide to American Art Song 1870–1980*. Lanham, MD, 1993, pp. 93–98. Teddy's most frequently recorded songs, dating from 1937, are the "Eight Epitaphs" that he took from poems by Walter de la Mare. Teddy's *Collected Songs* were published by G. Schirmer in the 1980s. The composer Ned Rorem wrote a glowing assessment of them in *Setting the Tone: Essays and a Diary.* New York, 1983, pp. 231–36.

10   In a letter to Hester discussing the China possibility Bebo wrote of Porter: "I think he's a bit cracked. All those sedentary years make it imperative for him to be super-duper active now that he is no longer a lawyer."

11   Sanche later became a Pulitzer Prize–winning journalist and author. In the 1960s he changed his name to Ted Morgan (an anagram of de Gramont). He was married briefly to a second cousin of mine, a granddaughter of Alida Emmet, one of the Astor orphans. We renewed our friendship with great pleasure a few years ago.

CHAPTER 11

Back in New York, 1945–52

I

N THE FALL OF 1945, WE RETURNED TO 108 EAST 82ND Street, I rejoined my class at Buckley (repeating 7th grade)[1] and Mary went back to the Brearly School. Most of my classmates had never left the city except to go to their summer homes in Connecticut and Maine or on Long Island. Their governesses were still picking some of them up after school, whereas I was trusted as I'd always been in Washington to make my own way on public transport. I noticed also that a few of the boys still said "wee-wee" while from my rougher schooling in Washington I knew how (rarely) to say "fuck," "shit" and "piss."

It was fun all the same to be reunited with them. I also loved the teaching at Buckley although I have forgotten who tried to teach me mathematics. I guess that the relentless Irish-American tribalism of Georgetown had gotten me down and I reverted happily to what I "was"—a jumpy, spotty, privileged, semi-WASP New Yorker.

My best friend at Buckley was Paul Mathews, whose father T.S. Mathews was then the editor of *Time* magazine and was also, without my knowing it at the time, the godfather of my future brother-in-law, Schuyler Jackson. I visited Paul at his parents' house in Newport in the. summers of 1946 and 1947 and then lost track of him for thirteen years.[2]

In 2010 I came across a patchy journal that I kept in 1946. It listed the books I read, my marks at Buckley, visitors to Westerly and my visits to school friends of mine in New England. One of the desultory entries, made on July 21 in Geneseo, reads: "Supper at Aunty Gertrude's [i.e. Sweetbriar]. Grandma's charecter [*sic*] torn apart." I doubt if Bebo's brother Hubert, then commanding a Naval Training Station fifty miles east of Geneseo, was present at the time, and I'd guess that Bebo and Gertrude reminisced about the problems of moving Daisy from the house in 1940 while Bebo, aided by martinis, took the opportunity to air some deeper resentments of her own.

That summer Bebo took me on a brief vacation to Northeast Harbor, Maine, and wrote Hester "lots of my friends are here which is very refreshing after the flab drab of Geneseo." I remember that Louis Auchincloss's first novel *The Indifferent Children* had just been accepted for publication and was the subject of vigorous conversations between Bebo and Louis's mother Priscilla, who spent her summers nearby in Bar Harbor. In a letter from Westerly to Daisy, Bebo wrote that the novel was "a disappointing book for a young man to have written ... I doubt if he ever does anything good." She changed her mind later on and came to admire Louis's work.

Bebo and Porter always intended to send me to boarding school after Buckley, which ended in eighth grade. In early 1946 I had a two-hour appointment in New York with a psychologist friend of Bebo's named Portia Hamilton to determine, among other things, where I should go. After a battery of tests, Dr Hamilton suggested that I attend a small boarding school and recommended Millbrook School in Millbrook, NY, which then had only a hundred boys and turned out to be an excellent choice.

Although barely fifteen years old, the school was heavily endowed and had a fine corps of teachers. I went there in September 1946 and graduated four years later in a class of thirty, rebonding with several of them at a 50th reunion weekend in 2000.

Bebo's life in this period was easier and more enjoyable than it had been for her in many years. Joe got out of the Navy in 1947, graduated from high school two years later and briefly enrolled in college. He married Ida Miller during a snowstorm in Geneseo in December 1950 and they settled in the village. Bebo was devoted to Ida and bonded with her four children, all born before Bebo died.

Judie had graduated from high school in 1947 and after a year of college began a career in hospital administration in New York. Mary and I, after 1948, were both away at school and in Mary's case, on a series of summer camps.

In these postwar years Bebo formed close friendships with several of her nephews and nieces, especially those who were in the process of getting married and having children. Beatrice's daughter Trixie, later Officer, was a special favorite. So were Peter and Jehanne White, Alida White and Jack Lessard and David and Betsy Pickman. They all remembered Bebo for her coziness, her wit and her unintrusive interest in their lives. Alida wrote me in 2002 that "Bebo was a very good aunt. I felt a real connection with her energy, which was such a fascinating mixture of a very real 'wake up and die right' and humor."

Seven years later when Alida knew I was working on this project she wrote: "Dear marvelous wild Bebo. She picked up winds that were carrying ideas and news of society's and religion's hunger and thirst, and she got involved with heart." Alida's sister Ann Buttrick, on the other hand, has written, "I never knew [Bebo] at all. She was always a remote, rather scary aunt."[3]

We moved back to 320 East 72nd Street in the fall of 1946,

when Porter purchased an apartment on the third floor that was smaller and darker than our twelfth-floor apartment had been. The apartment was our New York residence until 1959.

Starting in 1947, and until Bebo's death, Bebo and Porter were active in an ecumenical discussion group known as the Third Hour, which often convened in their apartment. The doorman at 320 once refused entry to the building to the poet W. H. Auden, a member of the group, because of his unkempt appearance. Anne Fremantle, Dorothy Day and the Russian author Helène Iswolsky were other members of the Third Hour, which numbered twenty to thirty people.[4] As Florence Davis has written:

> The exclusivity [of the Third Hour group] was never inten-
> tional; anyone who heard about the meetings and wanted to
> take part was welcome. By word of mouth, the group grew in
> numbers. Mrs. Porter Chandler, a wealthy American woman
> who knew France well, offered her large uptown apartment
> for the meetings. It was here that the Third Hour met for the
> coming years.[5]

In her published memoir, my cousin Martha Baltzell wrote that her aunt Bebo at this time

> worried about any show of extravagance with her Third Hour
> group. When she showed me two new attractive tables that
> she had just bought and set on either side of the fireplace in
> the living room, she said she feared being judged frivolous by
> her Third Hour friends. I attended a meeting of the group and
> remember a very sad, thin woman in her thirties with long
> stringy hair who looked close to despair. From my youthful
> perspective the other people seemed almost as depressed, and
> I never went again.[6]

According to Dorothy Day, on one occasion a truck driver

showed up at a Third Hour meeting in work clothes and when Bebo asked Dorothy who "this character" was Dorothy told her, "Bebo, we are all characters."[7]

As a teenager at boarding school and in college I occasionally looked in on Third Hour meetings but I didn't find the pious, elderly and seemingly lonesome people as depressing as Martha or my sister Mary did. In any case, the subject matter at the meetings was almost always over my head.

Bebo's Catholic activities and interests in the late 1940s and Porter's for that matter need to be placed in the context of the fervent religious revivals that flowed through the United States and other countries in the aftermath of World War II. The war had traumatized millions of its victims and participants. Veterans of the war, displaced persons and widows, among others, often found comfort and fulfilment in religious speculation and to a lesser extent in the religious life. Thomas Merton's influential autobiography *The Seven Storey Mountain* was published in 1948. It traced his intellectual pilgrimage to Catholicism and into a Cistercian (Trappist) monastery in the early 1940s.[8]

The Catholic Worker movement flourished at this time in the face of US government harassment and ecumenical movements such as the Third Hour gained adherents. Liberal Catholic journals such as *America*, the *Commonweal, Integrity* and *Jubilee* had a strong appeal to well-educated lay people secure in their beliefs who were also, for the most part, eager and even impatient for sweeping reforms to be enacted by the Church. Most of these men and women welcomed the far-sighted initiatives of Vatican II—as Bebo surely would have done—but once Pope John XXIII died, the more dramatic reforms they hoped for were never enacted.[9]

In 1949, putting his and Bebo's faith into action, Porter donated a 600-acre farm that he owned to the north of Westerly to the Cistercian Order. The Abbey of Our Lady of the Genesee was established in the following year. A handful of monks from the Gethsemani Abbey in Kentucky stayed at Westerly for several weeks until temporary, cloistered accommodation could be arranged at the site. For the rest of their lives Bebo and Porter followed the monastery's development attentively. It's still a flourishing institution with more than thirty resident priests and brothers. Bebo and Porter are buried on its grounds. In an undated letter to Daisy at about this time, Bebo wrote:

> Had a very vivid dream of being atom bombed. I behaved beautifully when I thought I would be killed instantly & went into a near panic when I was alone in the dark and knew the building was crashing over me. I got mixed up on my act of contrition but got through the Lord's Prayer OK. Was rescued by a man with a wheelbarrow.

The intellectual atmosphere in New York in the late 1940s, which Auden dubbed The Age of Anxiety, was coincidentally the heyday of film noir. These years included the religious revivals already mentioned, the insidious cross-currents of the Cold War alluded to in Bebo's dream and also, perhaps connected with both, the extraordinary surge of serious Broadway drama, including *A Streetcar Named Desire* and *The Death of a Salesman*, which I was fortunate to see with Bebo in their compelling original runs, as incidentally, as far as I knew Bebo and Porter didn't go to movies or the theatre together.

In the summer of 1948 Bebo translated two articles from German for *Commonweal*. In the first of these she noted that her "knowledge of German is limited to a three-month sojourn in Mecklenberg-Schwerin in 1912. This is therefore, of necessity, a so-called 'free translation.'" The second article, on socialism, was by the Italian writer Ignazio Silone and Bebo wrote Daisy that

"I only wish I had the original Italian." I remember her slaving over the translations. She never did any others. Bebo's isolation in Geneseo every summer continued to get on her nerves, especially now that her mother was no longer living nearby. As she wrote Daisy in June 1948:

> I don't dislike the country. I just feel frustrated by having no one to talk to about anything that matters. I find people who believe in nothing and didn't want to believe in anything terribly dull.

In those days Bebo didn't share these bouts of gloom with Porter, Mary or me, and I remember many happy times that Mary and I spent riding with her, learning to play tennis and playing croquet after dinner.

In the late 1940s, Mary began to excel academically at school and at competitive sports. She played tennis much better than I did, consistently trounced me at ping-pong and as a teenager starred on her boarding school's field hockey team. At other times, Bebo encouraged her to study the piano and taught her how to play bridge, a game that they both were good at and enjoyed. Mary inherited Porter's competitive drive and academic gifts alongside Bebo's talent for caustic, perceptive one-liners, but as she grew older she occasionally suffered from bouts of melancholia that she and I recognized were similar to Bebo's. These bouts became intense after Mary's divorce in 1971, and like Bebo's, were abetted by her drinking. In Mary's case, sadly, they weren't alleviated by any sustaining religious faith.

My memories of the late 1940s and early 1950s in Westerly are overwhelmingly pleasant and dusted with nostalgia. Often after dinner in those far-off days before TV (which an American journalist has aptly called a weapon of mass destruction) the four of us played charades and games that involved composing poems stanza by stanza (passed from person to person) or stories written paragraph by paragraph. Porter excelled at the poetry improvisations, turning out faux Victorian dirges that were impossible to "top". One memorable stanza ran:

"Bitter, bitter, hollow, hollow,"
Boomed the bittern, squeaked the swallow.
"Endless trouble, lonesome road,"
Chirped the sparrow, croaked the toad.

And this:

Home is the sailor, home from the sea.
Verses like this appeal to me:
Moral, significant, virtuous, bland.
Verses like this are especially grand.

Unless it was too hot, Mary and I went on two-hour horseback rides most afternoons with Bebo or on weekends with Porter. In 1948–50 we went cub hunting, the preliminary foxhunts of the season that were intended to train the hounds. For swimming, we could be driven to Conesus Lake or to swimming pools established in the 1950s at our Wadsworth cousins' house in Geneseo or at our friends the Cases in the nearby Avon. When Porter was in residence, we sometimes drove south into the Byersville hills for picnics in abandoned farms or visited Letchworth State Park where the Genesee River ran between steep gorges.[10]

I see now that the "feel" of these postwar years—except for the presence of electricity and automobiles—resembles what I've read about moderately privileged nineteenth – and twentieth-century English country life. When my friends Dick and Esther Eder visited Westerly in 1966, indeed, they told me that it reminded them of the Argentine *fincas*, where they had spent part of their childhoods in the 1930s and 1940s.

Was I bored? I can't remember. I maneuvered happily during those summers, often with Mary for company, and I wasn't ever bored in the same way that Bebo was. She missed the friends, varied activities and high-velocity conversations that she enjoyed in the city, while for me, totally taken care of, Westerly was a slow-moving Arcadian paradise with its green, cared-for vistas, enormous trees, horses to ride, ancestral resonances and lots of time for reading novels that Bebo recommended as well as outmoded children's books inherited from Porter and bound copies of the early twentieth-century children's magazine *St Nicholas*. A poem that I wrote about myself at Westerly in a slightly earlier era catches some of the flavor of those summer afternoons:

A Recollection
Midsummer 1944, soon after D Day,
I drifted back and forth
on a green porch swing
at ease, bemused, eleven and a half,
lost in a book from 1910
about the Zulu War.

It was my father's book. Perhaps in 1910,
eleven then himself, he'd also read
With Shield and Assegai
on the same wide porch
bemused like me,
hair parted on the right like mine.

In the wisteria filtered light
adrift, upstate, beside a sloping lawn
and far from Zululand or Normandy

I was as confident and pink
as a boy subaltern in 1910
with no one to command, obey or kill.

When I went off to Millbrook in September 1946, I soon learned that the way I spent my summers was different from the summers of many boys of my age and social position whose parents had houses in Connecticut or on Long Island where the boys could spend their summers meeting girls and learning to sail and dance. My social skills were slow to develop. They remain uneven to this day but my relatively solitary teenage summers at Westerly form an invaluable part of my life from which I draw fond memories, some crucial emotional balance and no regrets.

The summer of 1948 was important to my own development and my relationship with Bebo. Mary was away at camp that year, Judie was working in New York City and Joe was finishing high school in Connecticut. I spent a good deal of time alone with Bebo in Westerly. She taught me to type and was kind about the self-absorbed short stories that I banged out on her machine. Several of the stories concerned a sensitive 15-year-old boy marooned with his mother in a country house. Bebo also coached me in tennis and I paid enough attention to become a passable Sunday afternoon mixed-doubles player for another twenty years.

I see now that the close rapport that we enjoyed for the remainder of her life started in that remote, enjoyable summer. During my last two years at Millbrook that followed, Bebo coached me into reading her favorite writers. These included William Faulkner, F. Scott Fitzgerald, Graham Greene, Henry James, Evelyn Waugh, Rebecca West and Virginia Woolf. Some of her favourites were Faulkner's story "The Bear", Fitzgerald's *Tender is the Night*, Greene's *The Labyrinthine Ways*, published in England as *The Power and the Glory*, Waugh's Ethiopian novels and Woolf's *Journals*. Many years after her death I came to enjoy reading some of her French-language favourites, including Julien Green, François Mauriac and Jules Renard. Interestingly, she never championed Proust.

I happily accepted her suggestions and we always loved talking about books together. We enjoyed reading J.F. Powers' Catholic-oriented short stories and she steered me toward those of D.H. Lawrence and Katherine Mansfield.[11] These readings supplemented the excellent teaching of literature that I was receiving at Millbrook and made it inevitable, perhaps, that I majored in English when I went to college.

It's hard, all the same, to specify the elements of our intimacy that came into flower in 1948. Aside from books, we were both fond of amateur psychology, gossip, going to museums and movies, riding and (before long) playing tennis, smoking unfiltered cigarettes and drinking martinis together. I can't recall ever having an argument with her or any times when she was embarrassing or hard to talk to. Although she enjoyed what she may have called my "artistic temperament", she always hoped that I would take up a serious profession. Her advice, rarely given, always made excellent sense—a point echoed, when I was writing this memoir, by several of her nephews and nieces. At one point as a teenager I wrote her from school to say that I planned to live in the West Indies and "write". Her reply pointed out that such a "plan" would require a steady income and I quickly dropped it.

What was Bebo really like? Following the trail laid down by her letters and medical records, I've omitted many tangible details about her such as her appearance, her likes and dislikes and some of my specific memories. Bringing these to the surface at this stage of the book, drawing on the period when I knew her best, seemed a good idea and I was strongly encouraged to do so by my daughters Maggie and Liz.

Bebo was of average height, around five feet five inches. She had thick, light brown hair that became mixed with white and that she never dyed. She had pretty hands and a pleasant frame that became stockier with age. She moved gracefully. Her light blue eyes sometimes intimidated people who didn't know her or who failed to attract her interest. She had a fine color sense and a feel for fabrics, but she didn't enjoy shopping and spent relatively little time or effort on her clothes, although the colors she wore always suited her. She enjoyed and wore a few favorite pieces of jewelry.

Until the operations on her lungs in 1953 she was a good tennis player and a skilful rider. She also liked swimming and beaches, fresh vegetables and salad. In her fifties she came to enjoy cooking. For as long as I knew her, she liked strong coffee, Indian tea, martinis, bourbon whiskey, and Chesterfield cigarettes, but she was never a wine snob and unless there were guests the family drank decanted Gallo Zinfandel with dinner.

As mentioned, she loved going to movies and museums and devoted a good deal of her time to serious reading. Her religious life was also deeply important to her. I'd say that her greatest enjoyment, however, came from making and keeping friends and from lively conversation. She was curious and she was a good listener.

On the other hand, she could be abrupt and off-putting with people who failed to catch her attention. In 1937, therapists at Bloomingdale were told in a staff conference that "when she dislikes people, she cannot overcome her boredom." She also had little interest in the self-important aspects of the Chanler past, and had no time for flirtation, praise or flattery.

Taking a break from Bedford, Daisy spent part of the winters of 1947–49 in a rented apartment on East 84th Street in New York, where she had the services of a cook and a live-in nurse. I remember lunching with her there on two occasions in which I read her some of my jejune poetry. Louis Auchincloss has recalled several visits when he read aloud from the novels of Henry James. Bebo was delighted by Daisy's alertness and good humor. As she wrote to Hester:

> All goes well here and Mummy is wonderfully well. She finds Laura and me rather boring. I have only had 2 parties to describe to her at one of which I had a long conversation with Auden. She said, "He wouldn't be good for a salon."

I think Bebo wrote me about this conversation in which Auden, a friend of Anne Fremantle's since the 1930s, suggested that many of the crazier people of the Middle Ages might have been less mad if they been able to smoke.

In 1948 Anne arranged a lunch for Bebo and me at her apartment so I could meet Auden, whose poems I admired, but all I remember of the occasion is that he wore a leather jacket and wished me a "good term" at school. Through Anne, Bebo met several other literary figures in the late 1940s, including Graham Greene, Gore Vidal and Truman Capote. She wrote me amusing letters about these encounters.

On November 14, 1948 the English novelist Evelyn Waugh, passing through New York, wrote to his wife

> Next day I went … to the slums to see Dorothy Day an autocratic ascetic saint who wants us all to be poor, and her young men who are poor already & have a paper called *Catholic Worker* and a soup kitchen. I gave a great party of them luncheon in an Italian restaurant in the district & Mrs. Day didn't at all approve of their having cocktails or wine but they had them & we talked till four o'clock and then I went to tea with the leading Catholic lady of New York called Mrs.

Porter Chandler & Anne Fremantle was there and a deserted Catholic wife, very small and sad.[12]

Bebo never saw Waugh's accolade, of course, and I don't recall her telling me about the meeting.

In the summer of 1949, Bebo wrote to Daisy to recommend a biography of Abigail Adams, the wife of John Adams, the second president of the United States:[13]

> She is a distillation of all that is best in America & I never realized what a wonderful person her husband was. I have always been more interested in John Quincy. Henry Adams seems very *fin de race* in comparison … the weather is lovely here [Geneseo] and every prospect pleases but I find myself terribly boring! Social life seems to be a perpetual attempt to pull oneself up by one's bootstraps!

She closed the letter by saying: "Hester tells me you have made a real comeback since I left. I felt you were getting weaker by the minute when I was there. Perhaps daughters should stay away." In the fall, she contracted mumps, and ruefully wrote Hester:

> Oh, dear I am thankful this isn't the face the Lord gave me for life. It is too ugly for words & the awful part is it looks possible although not probable as a permanent face!

Soon afterwards, after lunching with Daisy in New York, she wrote to Hester:

> Mummy is in wonderful shape. She gave a bang-up lunch for Father d'Souza and Jean Seznec [a professor of French at Harvard]. Jean stared out with the dead eye of a Frenchman who is sure he's going to be bored. His eye got brighter and brighter when he realized how brilliant Father d'Souza was

(brighter than he was in fact)! I have never heard better conversation. Mummy was on the crest of a wave.

In the following summer, after my graduation from Millbrook, Porter, Bebo, Mary and I, accompanied by my cousin Deborah Pickman, travelled for two months in Europe. Beforehand, Bebo had written Hester:

> I think you should be sure Deborah has stout walking shoes for the mountains & comfortable *sight seeing* shoes. V. Important as I have gloomy memories of sore feet in conjunction with sight seeing.

Bebo flew to Italy with Mary and Deborah and settled into Forte dei Marmi on the Ligurian coast for a couple of weeks of rest and relaxation. The girls lolled on the beach, swam and went on bicycle rides as Bebo's childhood mastery of Italian came flooding back. They had spent time in Rome beforehand and had mounted expeditions to Lucca and other nearby sites, as Bebo told Hester in a long, happy letter.

Meanwhile, in June, Porter and I had flown the Atlantic. This must have been my first trip in a plane. We spent some time in England visiting Porter's friends and relatives in London and Oxford. I was pleased to see how happily he fitted back into English life, twenty-six years since his honeymoon visit. I noticed how easily several of his Balliol contemporaries rekindled their friendships with him. I got the feeling that for these friends and relatives it was almost as if Porter had never left. Through a seventeen-year old's fog of self-absorption I could see that his years at Oxford, which we visited briefly together, had been among the happiest in his life.

From England Porter and I went on to Paris where we joined my Millbrook classmate Martus Granirer, who was to travel with us as far as Rome. We picked up a small beige-colored Peugeot, which Porter, six feet 2½ inches tall, fitted into badly but drove very well as we travelled south. The tongue of the lion on the Peugeot's hood had been painted red, a touch that struck me at the time as particularly French. On the trip Porter took pains to take us through Chartres, Vézelay, Le Puy, Moissac and Avignon. We stayed at hotels or ate in restaurants whose food had been recommended by the Michelin guide. I'm convinced now that Porter, who was no food snob, arranged the itinerary at least in part to please two voracious, uninformed, food-snobbish boys. Driving into Italy, he skilfully negotiated hairpin turns on the Grande Corniche that hugged the cliffs beside the Mediterranean. I recall at one stage asking him to speed up. He declined. A moment later, two small, impetuous cars collided on the road ahead of us and Porter smiled triumphantly.

In Forte dei Marmi we reunited with Bebo, Deborah and Mary. Martus and I remember an excursion to the villa of the British expatriate writer Percy Lubbock, a friend of Daisy's and Edith Wharton's. Lubbock was out but his villa at Lerici, Gli Scafari, overlooked the spot in the Mediterranean where the poet Shelley had drowned. I remember staring down into the water.

Martus came to Rome with us for a few days before he flew back to New York. As a non-practicing Jew who was fond of Bebo and Porter, he was impressed and bemused by the enthusiasm with which we all responded as semi-pilgrims to the panoply of Holy Year in Rome.

From Rome we drove north into the Austrian Tyrol, stopping en route in Siena, Venice and Klagenfurt to stay for a week or so at a guesthouse in Igls, outside Innsbruck, to be near some Austrian friends of Bebo and Porter's, Erik and Christiane von Kuenheldt Leddihn. Erik (1909–1990) was a delightful Catholic libertarian and political commentator. He frequently stayed at our apartment when he came to America for lecture tours. In the late 1950s, Erik became the European editor for the *National Review*, a conservative American monthly.[14] From Austria we made excursions into US-occupied Germany and to nearby Baroque churches, whose ethereal whiteness and gilded carvings have stuck in my memory more firmly than many other things I saw that summer.

Porter flew back to work soon afterwards and Bebo heroically drove self-absorbed, incurious teenagers from Austria to Paris, where we spent a happy week in a friend's spacious apartment (with a resident cook) on the Avenue Victor Hugo, ten minutes walk from the much smaller flat that Susan and I rented on the Rue du Bouquet de Longchamps for seven months in 1992. In 1950 Bebo and the three of us dined on one occasion with the apartment's owners, Jehanne and Henri de Clarens, in their villa outside Paris. For two summers in the 1950s Mary worked for them as an au pair, improving her command of French.

This was Bebo and Porter's first time in Europe since 1933. The trip would certainly have been more enjoyable for them if they had not been saddled with Mary, Deborah and me but they conscientiously exposed us to the "sights," put up with what passed for conversation and did a good deal of strenuous driving. The trip gave us an excellent introduction to the continent that had played a major role in Daisy's life and to a lesser extent in Bebo's. I noticed fondly at the time that Bebo was delighted to reconnect with places and languages that she loved and to get a fleeting sense of postwar European culture and society.

I entered Harvard in September 1950, having been denied a favorable reference to Princeton because of the smoking offences that I'd committed at school. The offences turned out to have been blessings in disguise because I loved my years at Harvard. In my sophomore year as the Korean War (1950–53) dragged on

I took a physical examination for the Army that I passed despite my acute near-sightedness. In an era of universal military service, which remained in effect until 1973, the threat of being drafted hung over people my age with a special intensity because there were fewer of us born in the depths of the Depression than there were in any other age group in the US population. When our college deferments expired, we all expected to be drafted, and many of us were.

When I was in college, I took three summer jobs in New York City. In 1951, thanks to my classmate Peter Fisher, who had been an office boy at the *New Yorker* magazine the previous summer, I landed a similar job at the magazine for $25 a week. For a couple of months I enjoyed running messages between the offices of writers I admired and carrying edited manuscripts (by taxi) to other authors scattered around the city. This was the summer when J.D. Salinger's iconic novel *The Catcher in the Rye* appeared and I recall seeing Salinger, a tall, morosely handsome figure, several times in the *New Yorker* office.

In the following summer Peter and I travelled in Europe, armed with introductions to family friends in England, Austria, Spain, the Netherlands and France. Arriving in Southampton after crossing the Atlantic on the *Queen Mary*, we picked up two sturdy black bicycles at the Raleigh factory and cycled west to Devon and later around the château country in France.[15]

In the summers of 1953 and 1954, via an introduction to the publisher Robert Giroux by my cousin Peter White, I worked as an editorial assistant at the publishing firm of Harcourt, Brace for $40 (and in 1954 for $50) a week. Most of my work involved reading and almost always rejecting unsolicited manuscripts. I enjoyed being a small part of a very dedicated, talented team.

My three summers in the city threw me together with Porter and in some ways I got to know him and befriend him for the first time. We spent Monday to Friday together in 320 before heading off to Geneseo for the weekend. I enjoyed dining with him in restaurants or in his New York clubs, the Century and the Knickerbocker, occasions when our conversations exposed the riches of his alert, well-furnished mind; though this is not the way he would have expressed it. I absorbed a good deal of history, many family anecdotes and some amusing stories about his experiences as a corporate lawyer. We enjoyed walking to and from the Knickerbocker Club in the evenings and fixing breakfast every morning before we both set off for work.

On Friday nights in the summer of 1951 we set out at 11:00 PM in a bus from Rockefeller Center in Manhattan to the Erie Railroad terminal in Jersey City. It's hard explaining in 2020 why we wore jackets and ties for this nocturnal journey, even in the hottest weather, but none of the other passengers on the bus were casually dressed. The train left for Chicago a little after midnight.

The since defunct Erie Railroad was a client of Davis Polk and we travelled on Erie passes, which meant that we paid only for our Pullman berths. The nearest stop to Geneseo on the way from Jersey City to Chicago was Hornell, NY, about forty miles south of Westerly, a small city enshrined in the final sentence of F. Scott Fitzgerald's novel *Tender is the Night*.[16] Fitzgerald, a friend of Teddy's, visited Daisy and Teddy at Sweetbriar in the fall of 1927. Coming from Delaware where he was living at the time he may have driven through Hornell and stored the name away for later use.

In the summers of 1953 and 1954 after the financial collapse of the Erie we flew from La Guardia Airport to Rochester on Friday night—a faster but less enjoyable journey.

Porter's work at Davis Polk was largely in the field of antitrust litigation, where he defended such powerful clients as U.S. Steel, R.J. Reynolds Tobacco and J.P. Morgan. He wrote much of the brief for his partner John Davis's historic and successful argument before the Supreme Court that questioned the constitutionality of President Truman's seizure of America's steel mills in the course of a prolonged industrial dispute. He was also the lawyer for the Catholic Archdiocese of New York and argued several cases on its behalf before the Supreme Court. From 1951 until 1970, he served on the Board of Higher Education in New York City, becoming its chairman in 1966, when he sponsored an open admissions policy that was in character for Porter, a commonsense democrat, but was considered radical by many at the time.[17]

Bebo was always proud of Porter and she was always supportive of his career. In the early 1950s, however, he was embroiled in a massive, open-ended case in which it was his duty to prove to a judge's satisfaction that the United Fruit Company, a client of Davis Polk, was not a monopoly operating in restraint of trade, as anyone could see at a glance that it was. One evening at dinner Bebo, exasperated by the amount of Porter's time and energy that the case was taking, suggested to Porter that the company "Pay me a dollar and I'll go downtown to the judge and say, 'Just look at the record.'" Porter blanched, said something like "You can't do that!" and the case dragged on for several years. In 1952, I think, Bebo accompanied Porter and two of his partners to Guatemala for some onsite consultations with officials of United Fruit. She came home fascinated by the Guatemalan textile designs that she later incorporated into her weaving.

Daisy celebrated her ninetieth birthday quietly in Bedford in August 1952 and soon afterwards her health began to decline. To be near specialists and hospitals for the winter she moved to New York and although she had a full-time nurse in her hotel suite, Bebo was the primary carer and soon became exhausted by the work that needed to be done. She was also distressed by her mother's gradual loss of coherence. Daisy had always used her admirable, questing mind to impress strangers, maintain friendships and endear herself as an often-demanding intellectual companion to her children. Her mental decline, coming to her mercifully at ninety, was nonetheless a shock to Bebo and her siblings. Her death came quickly without much suffering in December 1952.

Notes

1   My grade-school education went from grades 1 to 5, then 7 and 8, followed by 7 and 9. I was almost a year younger than most of my classmates in college.

2   Schuyler Jackson (1934–) married my sister Mary in 1960. They had four children and divorced in 1971. Paul Mathews and I were ushers at their wedding.

3   When I tentatively embarked on this project in 1977 several of my first cousins, Daisy and Winty's grandchildren, recalled Bebo's courage, her gaiety, her skill at listening and her advice. They found her down to earth.

4   In a 1952 letter to Hester, Bebo wrote: "Am having what should be an interesting III Hour meeting … all French speaking, a French priest to talk. It will be full of what Mary calls my decadent royalty friends."

5   Florence Henderson Davis, "Lay Movements in New York City in the Forties and Fifties", *U.S. Catholic Historian*, vol. 9, no. 4 (1990), pp. 401–18. See also Helène Iswolsky, *No Time to Grieve: An Autobiographical Journey from Russia to Paris to New York.* Philadelphia, 1985, p. 250.

6   Martha Pickman Baltzell, *Bridging Diversity: Confessions of a Yankee Catholic.* New York, 1997, pp. 16–17. Third Hour meetings convened at our apartment until the winter before Bebo's death.

7   Undated notes from a conversation between Martha Baltzell and Dorothy Day, late 1970s.

8   On what has been called the "Catholic Renaissance " of the 1940s and 1950s see Garry Wills, "Shallow Calls to Shallow", *Harper's Magazine*, April 2019, pp. 78–82.

9   A liberal Catholic "wish list" envisaged allowing parish priests to marry and allowing non-ordained men to be appointed cardinals, a time-honoured practice that had never been formally abandoned. A relaxation of the Church's views of sexuality and reproduction was part of the wish list as well. The notion of women priests, however, had not yet arisen.

10 My 1946 journal mentions three Byersville picnics that summer, before the installation of the swimming pools mentioned above.

11 For an absorbing study of Powers and pre-Vatican II American Catholicism, see Paul Elie, "Bartleby in the Prairie: The Unspent Life of J.F. Powers", *Harpers Magazine*, September 2013. Bebo died too soon to know the work of Flannery O'Connor, whose bleak but compassionate Catholic point of view would certainly have appealed to her.

12 Mark Amory (ed.), *The Letters of Evelyn Waugh*. London, 1980, pp. 342–43. The "deserted Catholic wife" whom Waugh mentions was the sad woman Martha Baltzell remembered from a Third Hour meeting. I recall her too.

13 Janet Payne Whitney, *Abigail Adams*. Boston, 1947.

14 Erik was a close friend of my parents. In 1950 we stayed with his wife's parents in Klagenfurt, where his father-in-law, an Austrian count, had a large estate. The count had barely missed being arrested as a suspect in the plot to assassinate Hitler in 1944, six years before our visit.

15 In September 1954, I bought a similar Raleigh in Southampton and bicycled as far as Liverpool, where I took an overnight ferry to Dublin before bicycling for several days around Yeats country outside Sligo. I kept the bicycle during the academic year at Balliol that followed.

16 In the closing pages of the book its hero Dr Dick Diver is on a downhill slide in America after years of high living in Europe. In the final paragraph, Fitzgerald writes: "His latest note was post-marked from Hornell, New York, which is some distance from Geneva and is a very small town." On the visit to Geneseo, see Andrea Olmstead, *Who Was F. Scott Fitzgerald's Daisy?* no page number (ebook edition).

17 See "A Decisive Scholar", *New York Times*, December 20, 1966.

CHAPTER 12

Closing Off

DAISY'S FINAL MONTHS WERE DISTRESSING TO BEBO AND caused her to lose her mental balance once again. In the words of the records at Bloomingdale, where she was readmitted in February 1953, Bebo had recently

> developed more acute sleeping difficulties with nightmares, waking up screaming, becoming extremely concerned over simple problems, especially problems of ethics … She became very pious, going to Mass every day, began to worry about her increasing use of alcohol and cigarettes, finally called Dr Burdick about these problems and sought admission New York Hospital.

The admission form ticks boxes for "intemperate use of alcohol," "abnormal personality make-up" and "death of a relative" as causes for her admission. Her "personality" is listed as "unstable" and her "intellectual make-up" as "average." In April, as her condition improved, a therapist at Bloomingdale prepared a second report:

> On admission she was depressed, anxious, fearful and a little mixed up in her thinking. Psychoneurosis anxiety state seemed

a descriptive diagnosis, although she can move in and out of catatonic episodes. Her basic personality is that of an eccentric whose mind is bright but undisciplined and who has turned away from worldly values to spiritual ones. Her philosophy may be her protection against the strife and evil, which terrify her, and may also insulate her from the claustrophobia she feels in the female role of mother and wife.

Another doctor named Triebel, whom Bebo liked,[1] echoed some of these sentiments:

> Her relationship with both her mother and her husband has been markedly poor. Her mother was a cold, intellectual person who was able to give the patient very little and was indeed quite disappointed with the patient's attainments. Mrs Chandler appears to have made a struggle to live up to her mother's expectations of her and was, of course, never able to reach this impossibly high goal. She is a psychologist, rather intelligent person with fair insight into many of her difficulties, but she feels rather cornered by her home situation.

The phrase "markedly poor" for Bebo's relations with Porter strikes me as an exaggeration, but it probably reflects some intemperate statement, absent from her medical records, that Bebo made at the time. Interestingly, none of the records refers to menopause, which she must have been enduring at about this time and none of them (aside from her admissions details) deals with her abuse of alcohol that by the 1950s had become less constrained than before. It soon became clear to me also that Bebo had become an alcoholic. Porter was distressed by this, but was unable to do anything about it.

An unnamed doctor, searching for an appropriate diagnosis, wrote: "She has been an eccentric all her life and eccentric people have peculiar illnesses." I agree with this assessment in the sense that Bebo was always "off-centre" as far as many people were concerned, but in a wider context I don't think her illnesses were especially "peculiar."

On another occasion in an exchange with a Dr Moss, Bebo said, "I'm afraid of insanity" and when Dr Moss replied, "Do you have any explanation for this illness of yours?" Bebo said, "It's something that runs in my family, but unfortunately Dr Burdick does not agree with me on that point."

Bebo arrived at the hospital anxious, unsteady and in a high fever. Over the next few weeks she responded favorably to bed rest and to formal interviews with members of staff. In the process she became more outgoing. On March 25 Dr Triebel reported that

> She has become interested in several patients, is friendly and sociable toward them and has been particularly interested in Miss Deneger, a catatonic, schizophrenic patient with whom she seems to have developed a good relationship.

On the whole Bebo was less happy with her treatment at the facility in 1953 than she had been in 1937. She made bold requests for the Bible and a book by the psychiatrist Alfred Adler (1870–1937), a rival of Sigmund Freud. The requests were refused on the grounds that the books were inappropriate. She presumably would have sought comfort in the Bible and some help in self-analysis from Adler but arguments from either source with her therapists would not have been on their agenda. She wrote to Hester impatiently, "They are doing everything by charts and electronics nowadays and it all seems more remote than ever before from anything that matters to me."

She knew, however, that she was once again in safe hands and that she needed to be removed for a time at least from the pressures of her family, from the impact of Daisy's death and perhaps from her addictions. In later years, my sister Mary was fearful that Bebo had received electric shock therapy during her sojourns in White Plains but Dr Steven Roth, when I asked him about this, assured me that this treatment was not used at the hospital in either 1937 or 1953.

Happily, as part of her therapy at Bloomingdale in 1953 Bebo developed a skill at weaving that nourished her for the remainder of her life. While she was still a patient at Bloomingdale, she underwent surgery in New York City to remove a cancer in one of her lungs and had a lobe removed. The condition was clearly connected with her addiction to cigarettes. She was released provisionally in the late spring of 1953 and returned for checkups and brief visits for the remainder of the year and into 1954.

In this period of her life, Bebo made two new friends who would become important to her. The first was Ivan Illich (1926–2002), an intense, inspiring Austrian priest who was then working in a largely Puerto Rican parish in Washington Heights at the northern tip of Manhattan. The second friend was Catharine Carver (1921–1997), then a junior editor at the publishing house Harcourt, Brace.

When Bebo learned that Ivan had been born in the same year as my dead brother John, they developed a moving mother–son relationship as well as a teacher–student one, with Bebo eagerly responding to Ivan's friendship and to his rigorous readings, shared with her, from some stiff theological texts, mostly in German, and of parts from the Old Testament.

Ivan and I also became close friends and I worked with him for several months in Puerto Rico in 1958. When Susan and I were planning to be married nine years later, I asked him if he could perform the ceremony. As an alert, baptised Lutheran, Susan was understandably wary of Catholic proselytizing but Porter's religious fervor and my own lingering faith made it psychologically impossible for me to marry outside the Church. Happily, Ivan told us that he would be delighted to perform the ceremony. He suggested that it take place at CIDOC, the think tank he was running at the time, loosely affiliated with the Catholic Archdiocese of New York, in the Mexican city of Cuernavaca. Susan and I were married there in June 1967 in a convivial, open air, interdenominational ceremony.

Ivan left the priesthood two years later after prolonged and heated confrontations with the Catholic hierarchy in Mexico, New York and Rome. He embarked on a career as a polemicist, attacking what he saw as an iatrogenic or patient-killing medical profession, an inhumane educational establishment and what he considered to be the ahistorical rigidities associated with radical feminism. Ivan's courageous, innovative positions, partially anchored in Utopia, lost traction with the public in the 1980s and he spent the last twenty years of his life teaching medieval intellectual history and writing about it in congenial universities in Germany and Pennsylvania.

Ivan was our daughter Maggie's godfather and he visited us in Geneseo before we went to Thailand in 1970. After that we lost touch and we seldom saw him, except for a flying visit that he made to Melbourne to give lectures in 1978. In 2001, when Susan and I were living in Washington, DC, Ivan dropped by unexpectedly for dinner and the night. He was very ill with cancer and, as always, he was refusing medical attention. Although he was in considerable pain, we spent a nostalgic evening together and we drove him out to rural Maryland in the morning to a house where he was staying. He died in Germany a few months later. As an inspiring, unofficial older brother, Ivan was an enormous influence on me.[2]

In the summer of 1953, when I befriended her, Catharine Carver was a junior editor at Harcourt, Brace and a respected critic. An Irish American, she was also what we might call today a recovering Catholic. More importantly, she was a person of intense intelligence, empathy and integrity. At my request, Bebo invited her to dinner at the apartment on several occasions when I was in New York. The two of them "hit it off" at once and as Louis Auchincloss wrote in his letter to me about Bebo:

> I think "abrupt capacity for friendship" is a good phrase in any description of your remarkable mother. She was shrewdly perceptive and could spot a responsive intellect or heart in a flash.[3]

Caty was devastated when Bebo died and wrote me a thoughtful letter about their friendship. I had worked closely with her in the summers when I was at Harcourt, Brace. Thanks to her I was the second person to read the manuscript of William Gaddis's quirky, path-breaking novel *The Recognitions*, which she had obtained for the firm. In 1956 Bebo asked Gaddis, his wife and Caty to dinner at 320 on a weekend when I was there and in the late 1950s she sometimes assembled small, "literary" dinners for me featuring such guests as Louis Auchincloss, my Harvard classmate John Updike, who was then working at the *New Yorker*, and John McGiffert, my former English teacher at Millbrook, who was making a name for himself in New York TV. Unfortunately, I never saved any of the "story games" that we played after the dinners.

Whenever I was in New York in those years Bebo and I traipsed off together to the movies, MOMA, the Frick Collection, the Cloisters or the Metropolitan Museum. We often lunched at her club, the Cosmopolitan on East 66th Street, where she had many friends. On my twenty-first birthday in 1954 she took me to Brooks Brothers to buy me a dark grey suit, which I wore until I was thirty, and to a watchmaker to buy a fine Swiss watch that lasted with lots of hard use until 1966.

In the fall of 1953 as I began my senior year at Harvard, Mary entered Radcliffe, Harvard's sister college. She graduated in 1957. Like Porter, we were both taken into the honor society Phi Beta Kappa but neither of us graduated at the head of our class.

That Christmas, Mary "came out" as a debutante in New York and Bebo wrote Hester: "We gave an enormous dinner for Mary and her friends. The poor maids didn't leave until 11:45! How unconscious we used to be about that sort of thing!" It's clear that while she was still an outpatient, Bebo was doing the best she could as a mother.

Just before my graduation in June 1954, Bebo was so engrossed watching the so-called Army-McCarthy hearings on TV that she inadvertently knitted part of a third sleeve onto a sweater destined for one of Joe and Ida's children. I learned from her medical records that she was then on a provisional six-month release from Bloomingdale. Dr Burdick noted at the time: "Diagnosis: psychoneurosis, anxiety states. Condition: Much improved."

For the remainder of the year she continued to visit Dr Burdick in the Manhattan offices of the hospital. In October, Dr Burdick reported that Bebo "has had less tension and only fleeting delusions which she recognizes as such and some visual experiences which have been distressing but controllable." In May 1955, just before she left for a trip to Europe, Bebo received her final discharge from Bloomingdale. The form read "Much improved" and "Without psychosis", but as in 1938 the box "Recovered" wasn't checked.

I spent the academic year 1954–55 at Balliol College, Oxford, where, among other things, I befriended the sons of several scholars who had been there with Porter in the 1920s. I also rowed in an Eight and in the spring vacation I travelled to Italy and

Greece with a Harvard classmate, Douglas Macneal. Bebo and Porter visited me in Oxford in June and we went on from there to Ireland, where we stayed with some of Porter's Anglo-Irish relatives. Before coming to England Bebo had spent several weeks in Madrid boarding with a family to improve her Spanish. In August Bebo wrote Dr Burdick from Stonington, Connecticut, where she had rented an apartment for a month:

> This place has turned out to be ideal. Very nice people & wonderful weaving. There is a lady who lives here all the year round and is the best weaver I've met. She has given me the run of her looms and material besides teaching me a whole lot of wrinkles. This has made it possible for me to really keep in good shape.[4]

For the next three years, Bebo spent two or three weeks every summer in Stonington, where some of her New York friends had summer houses and where she enjoyed living near the beach, two hours by train from New York City. As she wrote Hester from Stonington in August 1955, "The people here couldn't be nicer to me. Just my style of social life."

In that same month I decided for several reasons not to return to Balliol. More academic work or living in England for another year did not appeal to me and I was liable for military service, so when I came home to Geneseo I volunteered for the draft—in effect shortening my time in the queue—and was told that I would be drafted in late October, a few weeks after Judie's wedding in St Felicity's to Robert Houston. Like Joe and Ida, Judie and Bob settled happily in the town of Geneseo and raised a family there.

I spent the next two years as an enlisted man in the Army, mostly as a clerk in the Pentagon, a posting that enabled me to get up to New York for most weekends.[5] At some point in 1956, Bebo wrote to Hester:

Re-reading my old letters has made me terribly self-conscious. I see (when we decide on the final disposal of family letters) saying to myself, "I haven't changed at all!"—I think it's actually quite depressing to "*constater*" that as Pick so wisely observed in his historical studies. At 25 one has pickled into one's generation & can be dated accordingly no matter how much one may dream of having made something rich and strange & different of oneself with the passing of years. The only word I would no longer use is "nigger." The opinions are the same. Perhaps a touch mellowed. David who was here last weekend picked out a lot at random and was horrified to see how early I'd jelled. He could see no change in point of view at all. So, I guess I'm less fascinating than I'd hoped![6]

Bebo at Westerly c1957

On several occasions in the 1950s, Bebo and Porter visited Hester and Pick, who leased a cottage every winter on the grounds of the Mill Reef Club on the island of Antigua, then still part of the British West Indies. Other guests at the club included Dean and Alice Acheson, friends from the 1920s, and the poet Archibald MacLeish.

While her physical health declined in the late 1950s and included a second operation on her lung in 1957, Bebo's mental balance and morale improved significantly. In a note following one of her visits to Dr Burdick's office in 1957, for example, the doctor wrote that "She has many interests and is travelling about a good deal."

In the spring of that year, when I was still in the Army, I hitched a ride on a military aircraft and spent ten days in London and three in Paris where my uncle Teddy had been living at the St James and Albany Hotel on a kind of sabbatical after the critical success of his one-act opera, *The Pot of Fat*, based on a Grimm fairytale, "The Cat and Mouse in Partnership", for which his sister Hester had written the libretto.

I had always liked my uncle but we hadn't spent much time together. Those three days with him were a delightful, bonding experience. Teddy took me to visit Alice Toklas and Nadia Boulanger, his former teacher, to whom he introduced me as "*mon neveu le poète.*" We attended a Lorca play and ate a sumptuous lunch in a restaurant near the Palais-Royal that had been favored by my uncle Larry White. We walked for miles and miles. I don't recall taking the Metro. This was the closest I had come to Paris (or to Teddy, for that matter) and when I lived in the city later on, I often recalled those three days with pleasure. I loved our conversations but I've forgotten what we said. Later that year, as we'll see, Teddy visited us in Geneseo.

In the meantime, a US Foreign Service officer named John

McVickar, whom I'd met in Washington through mutual friends, had drawn me toward the idea of joining the Foreign Service, a career prospect that pleased my parents. In June 1957, I took the written examinations for the service and learned soon afterwards that I had passed. Up until then I'd assumed that I would follow several of my Harvard classmates into the publishing business in New York. I considered myself a "writer" without having published anything commercially and I now felt that a diplomatic career would support my writing habit and increase my writer's capital in ways that working for a publishing house in New York City might not. My diplomatic career lasted eight years and as I've written elsewhere my first overseas posting to Cambodia in October 1960 changed the direction of my life.[7]

In September 1957, Teddy visited us in Geneseo for a few days and he and Bebo enjoyed a close, almost manic reunion. I remember their spending an afternoon together reading Paul Valéry's *M. Teste* aloud to each other and (behind closed doors) bursting into bouts of laughter that were inspired, I suppose, by happy memories and by the off-center, private sense of humor that they had always shared. It was a joy for me to see and hear the two of them together.

I passed the oral examination for the Foreign Service in New York in November 1957 and learned at the time that US government budget constraints would keep me from being sworn in for almost another year. Cooling my heels in the city, I finally learned to drive. My AAA lessons took me to West End Avenue in Manhattan, which, as an Upper East Side provincial, I had very rarely seen.

For the first seven months of 1958 I worked at the Catholic University of Puerto Rico in the city of Ponce where Ivan Illich was the vice-rector. I acted as Ivan's personal assistant and also ran an adult education program, in which I arranged for a wide curriculum and gave short courses myself on Greek tragedy (which I'd studied in college) and the modern novel (which I hadn't). In the summer I worked with Ivan on a two-month-long workshop for about twenty Catholic priests brought down from the New York archdiocese. They were eager in most cases to learn more about Hispanic culture and about Catholicism as it was practiced in Puerto Rico. Cardinal Spellman, the Archbishop of New York, paid an official visit to the project at one stage.

I remember many conversations with Ivan in which he was cautiously optimistic about the possibility of dramatic changes in the Catholic Church. His contacts with liberal theologians and liberal elements in Rome and elsewhere convinced him that sweeping changes were not far off, but would depend on the election of a less conservative pope than Pius XII. His hopes like those of many were later dashed.

In March, coming from a visit to the Pickmans in Antigua, Bebo visited us in Ponce and went on to Florida to stay with her friend Alida Conover, who had enjoyed a successful artistic career, largely as an illustrator, and was no longer as passionately on the left.

Bebo wrote me in Ponce in July. This is only letter from her that I seem to have saved. After mentioning that Judie was entranced with her new baby, she wrote:

> I am getting better and better by the minute. I actually didn't think about it at all when I picked up [Joe's wife] Ida to take her and [her daughter] Martha to the oculist in Warsaw [a nearby village]. On the way home I suddenly realized how much better I was as two weeks ago I had to go to buy paint and made arrangements for Gertrude [Chanler] to drive me there!

I came home at the end of August and visited Bebo in

Stonington. I remember going to a beach in nearby Rhode Island with her and shopping together for summer clothes. We had cocktails with friends of Bebo's from New York and we ate meals that Bebo prepared very well. She showed me some of her recent sketches and pastels, which struck me as excellent. As with Teddy in Paris, we must have talked and talked but I can't remember anything we said.

After a few days together, we packed up the gray Buick sedan that Bebo had chosen for the family in 1951 and set off on the daylong journey to Geneseo. About halfway there Bebo stopped the car and asked me to drive. This surprised me because she was an excellent driver and loved to drive.

In clearing out her Stonington apartment we had packed a few cans of beer into the Buick. When she stopped the car Bebo drank one of them by the side of the road—thirstily, as if something was wrong with her that was connected with her asking me to drive. Hindsight is at work here but the image of her drinking that can of beer remains more sharply in my head than do many other moments of my life. The rest of the trip with me at the wheel was uneventful.

After a day or two with Bebo in Geneseo, I drove to Washington in Mary's small gray Saab to rent an apartment and to find out about being sworn in as a Foreign Service Officer Class 8. This was the first time I'd driven along US Route 15, which later became one of my favorite highways in America.

My memories of the next few days are full of empty spaces. I know that I found and rented (for $100 a month) a pleasing furnished apartment on the top floor of a house overlooking Rock Creek Park in Northwest Washington. I also learned that my orientation was scheduled to begin in about ten days. I drove back to Geneseo, eager to tell Bebo what had happened and what lay in store for me.

At lunch the next day she looked at me across the table and said, with an unfamiliar note of urgency, "I can't remember anything any more." I immediately made an appointment for her to see a doctor in Geneseo named Julia Delahunty, whom Bebo had always respected. Julia examined her and told me that Bebo's aphasia might be symptomatic of brain cancer. This turned out to be the case. Julia urged me to drive her that afternoon to the Strong Memorial Hospital in Rochester, promising in the meantime to make the appropriate telephone calls.

At Westerly we packed a bag for her and I telephoned Porter in New York. I remember nothing about the journey by car to Rochester, which took about an hour in those days. What did we talk about? Did it occur to me that she was dying?

Porter flew up to Rochester the next day and we visited Bebo in the hospital together before coming home to Westerly. At Strong Memorial, Bebo was diagnosed with an inoperable brain cancer that had metastasised from the cancer discovered earlier in her lung.[8] At that point it seemed best to move her to New York City in an ambulance, and this was done around September 10. By then she was immobile and almost speechless.

Over the next few weeks I was only able to visit her on weekends as my Foreign Service career, which had begun when she returned to New York, gathered momentum. My memories of visiting her are a blank in part because it was hard to enter her illness into my consciousness alongside my excitement at embarking on a career. I was also unable and unwilling to process what was going on because the weeks before she died and a few months thereafter coincided with a romantic involvement that had sprung up for me in New York.

I have always been ashamed of my behavior toward Bebo in her dying days and I only hope that in my visits to 320, where I came home to sleep, I gave some support to Porter. I'm glad to say that Mary, who was working at the time in Cambridge, Massachusetts, also came to New York every weekend.

Other visitors wrote to Porter as encouragingly as they could. Hester noted that Bebo had "gotten off a few sentences" to her, while Beatrice wrote that her younger sister had "laughed at little jokes." Bebo's last two months were probably cruel for someone who throughout her life had been "over-productive verbally", in the words of a therapist in 1953, but the end was always in sight, she was never in pain and Ivan Illich wrote Porter in October that he prayed "every day at Mass for a beautiful death for Bebo."

In late October Porter summoned me home from Washington. A priest must by then have come to the apartment and delivered the sacrament of Extreme Unction, sometimes known as the Last Rites. On October 25, forewarned by the nurse, Porter, Mary and I were on our knees at Bebo's bedside reciting decades of the Rosary when she died at 7:30 AM. The family doctor, Dr Neergaard, was called in to sign the death certificate. Funeral home employees removed Bebo's body from the apartment soon afterwards in a black rubber bag. She had never been in a freight elevator before.

For the next few days Bebo's body lay in a closed coffin in Campbell's Funeral Home on Madison Avenue as Porter made arrangements to ship the remains by train to Geneseo. In those days there was still a nine-hour-long passenger service operated by the Lackawanna Railroad between Hoboken, New Jersey and Buffalo that stopped at the village of Mount Morris a few miles south of Geneseo. Porter and I accompanied the coffin on one such train in the closing days of October. Two days later she was buried on the grounds of Our Lady of the Genesee. The funeral High Mass at the monastery was sung in the so-called Church Latin that Bebo and Porter knew and loved. Porter was buried beside her in 1979. Their graves, like Westerly, look east across the Genesee valley.

Touchingly, and ahead of his time, Porter had Bebo's tombstone inscribed with her maiden name.[9] For the words, he chose four verses from the Book of Proverbs, Chapter 31. They were inscribed in Latin. In English, the verses read:

> 26. When she opens her mouth, she does so wisely.
> 11. Her husband's heart has confidence in her.
> 28. Her children stand up and proclaim her blessed.
> 31. Let her works tell her praises at the city gates.

A memorial service for Bebo in New York a couple of weeks later drew a crowd of her friends and relatives to a High Mass at St Ignatius on Park Avenue at 84th Street, a baroque-style Jesuit church that she and Porter had sometimes attended. Several priests officiated at the ceremony, including Andrew Rogosh and Ivan Illich. Back at the apartment afterwards we heard on the radio that a promising new Pope, John XXIII, had just been elected.

In the November 1958 issue of the *Catholic Worker*, Bebo's old friend Dorothy Day wrote:

> This morning we went to the Liturgy at St. Michael's chapel on Mulberry street where we usually meet Helène Iswolski on a Sunday morning, and Anne Marie Stokes who sings in the choir. This morning after the liturgy of the Mass, there were the prayers for the dead, very movingly sung. Fr. Rogosh spoke of the great charity of Gabrielle Chandler who had also been a benefactor of The Catholic Worker since the very earliest days. She first came to see us when we had our office on Fifteenth Street, and she and her husband paid the rent for the women's house of hospitality for the first year. We were lodged then in an apartment down the street from the office. One of the more recent acts of tenderness was her buying a crib for the eighth baby of a needy Negro family. Fr. Rogosh

told how when the Russian chapel was getting under way, Gabrielle Chandler and her husband Porter came to help him clean on Saturdays, in preparation for the liturgy. Also, how she helped many Russians who were in need. What a consoling thought, "their works follow them." She suffered a great deal, and one can only rejoice the she has now a place of refreshment, light and peace.

Notes

1   In an undated letter to Hester from the hospital Bebo noted that she "had a good talk with Dr Triebel who is much quicker on the trigger and far more cultivated than Dr Burdick. He is also not an old maid which helps too and he loves to laugh."

2   On Illich, see David Cayley, *Ivan Illich in Conversation.* Toronto, 1992; and Ivan Illich and David Cayley, *The Rivers North of the Future: The Testament of Ivan Illich as told to David Cayley.* Toronto, 2004, which discusses Ivan's life and ideas in detail.

3   Louis Auchincloss, letter of August 6, 2000. The phrase "abrupt capacity for friendship" was mine, taken from the letter that Louis was answering.

4   Bebo's letter was included in her medical records.

5   Without my knowledge Porter pulled strings among former colleagues in the Pentagon to remove me from a Quartermasters Corps assignment, which might have taken me to Germany. I resented Porter's well-intentioned interference at the time but I couldn't do anything about it. My subsequent Pentagon assignment, as things turned out, led me indirectly onto my career paths in civilian life.

6   The letters Bebo refers to would have been ones that she wrote to Porter. She never made copies of her other letters and the ones that she wrote to Daisy and Hester, cited so often in these pages, didn't come to my attention until several years after she died.

7   See my essay "Coming to Cambodia", in Anne Hansen and Judy Ledgerwood (eds), *At the Edge of the Forest: Essays on Cambodia, History and Narrative in Honor of David Chandler.* Ithaca, NY, 2008, pp. 21–28.

8   Lung cancer traceable to a lifetime of smoking also killed my two sisters, Mary and Judie, in their sixties.

9   In transmitting family papers to the New York Historical Society in 1974, Porter described Bebo as a "talented artist, linguist and horsewoman." In similar circumstances, I wonder now, what would I have said?

Acknowledgments

OVER THE TEN YEARS THAT I HAVE BEEN WORKING ON this memoir, many of my relatives and friends provided thoughtful comments, sometimes given more than once, and often in early drafts. I'm especially grateful to my late wife Susan for making me think through what I was trying to say and for helping me to arrange the material in its present form.

I'm also happy to acknowledge the helpful comments that came to me at various stages from Louis Auchincloss, Louis Begley, Janet Butler, Ann Buttrick, James Case, Liz, Maggie and Tom Chandler, Ida Chandler, Nicholas Clifford, Graeme and Barbara Davison, Catherine Drew, Campbell and Margot Flack, Austin Flint, Susan Foley, David Garrioch, Katherine Gilmour, Joan Grant, Martus Granirer, Aleida White Hare, Philip, Maria, Kathy and Celia Jackson, Cynthia Jay, Peter Judd, Walter Kaiser, Ben LaFarge, Alfred McCoy, Margaret and James McLeish, Jim Mitchell, Ted Morgan, Claire Murray, Seth Mydans, Brenda Neall, Andrea Olmstead, Mary Procter, Craig Reynolds, Mark Schwartz, Nicholas Shakespeare, Charles Sowerwine, Michael Train and Hiram W. Woodward, Jr.

I am especially grateful to Ian Britain and Cathie Drew for their close and helpful reading of the final text, and to Richard McGregor for his fastidious and highly professional copyediting.

Acknowledgments

In the memoir I have drawn on papers in my possession and on those housed in the New York Historical Society in New York City. I'm grateful to the librarians Tami Kiter and Ted O'Reilly for their help when I visited the society's archive in 2008, 2010, 2012 and 2019.

I am grateful to Kerr Publishing for shepherding the manuscript into print, and to Paul Taylder for giving the book its pleasing appearance.

Bebo's Nuclear Family

Winthrop Astor Chanler (Winty, 1863–1926) married Margaret Terry (Daisy, 1862–1952) in 1886. After 1904 they lived primarily in "Sweetbriar" in Geneseo, New York. They had eight children, seven of whom survived to adulthood:

1. Laura Astor Chanler (1887–1984) married Lawrence Grant White (Larry),* an architect, in 1916. They had eight children. The only child surviving in 2021 is Cynthia.* Her deceased siblings were Peter,* Elizabeth, Aleida,* Robert, John, Sarah and Ann.* From 1938 onward, the Whites lived in St James, Long Island, New York.

2. John Winthrop Chanler II (1889–1893) died in a sledding accident in Tuxedo Park, NY.

3. Beatrice Margaret Mary Chanler* (1891–1974) married Pierre Allegaert,* a jeweller, in 1923. Beatrice became deaf at the age of three following a bout of scarlet fever. Her husband was deaf from birth. They had three children: Francis,* who was killed as an infantryman in central France in World War II, Beatrice (Trixie)* and Winthrop (Win),* who both died in 2018. The Allegaerts lived in Newton, Massachusetts and Laconia, New Hampshire.

4. Hester Marion Chanler (1893–1990)* married Edward Motley Pickman* (Pick), an historian, in 1915. They had six children: Anthony, Margaret (Daisy), Jane, David,*

Martha* and Deborah*. They lived in Boston and in Bedford, Massachusetts. Only Martha was still alive in 2020.

5. Marion Winthrop Chanler (1895–1931)* was mentally impaired and never married. He lived in Plymouth, Massachusetts.

6. May Margaret Gabrielle Chanler (Bebo) (1897–1958)* married Porter Ralph Chandler,* a lawyer, in 1924. They had five children, four of whom survived into adulthood: John, who died shortly after his birth, Joseph (Joe),* Judith (Judie),* David,* the only survivor in 2021, and Mary*. They lived in "Westerly" in Geneseo, New York and in New York City.

7. Hubert Winthrop Chanler (1900–1974),* a career US Naval officer. He married Gertrude Laughlin* in 1937. The couple had eight children, six of whom survive: Elizabeth,* Alexander, Felicity, Gay and Alida. Their son John Winthrop Chanler died in 2008, and Oliver* died in 2016. After Hubert's retirement from the Navy in 1952, the family lived in Geneseo, NY, Washington, DC and New York City.

8. Theodore Ward Chanler (Teddy)* (1902–1961), a composer and critic, married Maria de Acosta Sargent in 1931. They lived in New York City, and in Boston, Ipswich and Harvard, Massachusetts.

*Mentioned by name in the text.

APPENDIX B

Bernard Berenson's Diary
Entry on Daisy's Death

"Daisy" Chanler is dead, the last of my contemporaries. Was a survivor of a generation prior to mine intellectually, although she could have been at most three years only my elder? Daughter of a missionary [*sic*] and a snobbish mother, brought up in Rome to the cult of Roman high society, she naturally ended as a Catholic. Yet being American, she took her religion too seriously, and handed it on to all her offspring to the fourth generation. There was something expansive, generous, radiant about her, and a perpetual adolescence of mind that made her eager for contact with what she could follow and try to assimilate in what was going on in the upper reaches of recent but already consecrated literature and art. A great reader, in German as well of course in Italian and in French, she was like Edith Wharton, with whom one could discuss any book of European interest—but never on the sociopolitical plane.

REFERENCES

Alexandra Aldrich, *The Astor Orphans*. New York, 2013

Mark Amory (ed.), The *Letters of Evelyn Waugh*. London, 1980

Carolyn Anthony (ed.), *Family Portraits*. New York, 1980

Louis Auchincloss, "Edith Wharton and Margaret Chanler", in his *Love Without Wings: Friendships in Literature and Politics*. New York, 1991, pp. 47–58
——*A Voice from Old New York: A Memoir of My Youth. New York, 2011*

Paul Baker, *The Fortunate Pilgrims: Americans in Rome, 1800–1860*. New York, 1965

Sir John Balfour, *Not too Correct an Aureole: Recollections of a Diplomat*. London, 1983

Martha Pickman Baltzell, *Bridging Diversity: Confessions of a Yankee Catholic*. New York, 1997

Iven Bernstein, *The New York City Draft Riots*. New York, 1990

R.P. Blackmur, *Henry Adams*. New York, 1980

J. Sanbourne Bockhoven MD, "Moral Treatment in American Psychiatry", *Journal of Nervous and Mental Disease*, vol. 124 (1956), pp. 167–94 and 292–321

Ann Buttrick, "Box Hill", unpublished memoir, 2018

Anne Canavan, "Was Daisy an Astor?", *The F. Scott Fitzgerald Review* (2013), pp. 173–77

David Cayley, *Ivan Illich in Conversation*. Toronto, 1992

John Armstrong Chaloner, *Four Years behind the Bars at Bloomingdale*. Roanoke NC, 1906

David Chandler, "Coming to Cambodia", in Anne Hansen and Judy Lidgerwood (eds), *At the Edge of the Forest: Essays on Cambodia, History* and Narrative in Honor of David Chandler. Ithaca, NY, 2008

Porter R. Chandler, *Anniversary Requiem for GC*. New York, 1963
——*"How My Grandfather almost Lost the Civil War"*, *American Neptune 33* (January 1973), pp. 5–15

Mrs Winthrop Chanler, *Roman Spring*. Boston, 1934
——*Autumn in the Valley*. Boston, 1936

Margaret Chanler, *Memory Makes Music*. New York, 1948
——*(ed.), Winthrop Chanler's Letters*. New York, 1951

Susan Chitty (ed.), *As Once in May: The Early Autobiography of Antonia White*. London, 1983

Deborah Pickman Clifford, *Mine Eyes Have Seen the Glory: A Biography of Julia Ward Howe*. Boston, 1976

Lisa Cohen, *All We Know: Three Lives*. New York, 2012

Georgina Pell Curtis (ed.), *Some Roads to Rome: Being Personal Records of Conversion to the Catholic Church*. St. Louis, 1911, pp. 83–4

Florence Henderson Davis, "Lay Movements in New York City in the Forties and Fifties", *U.S. Catholic Historian*, vol. 9, no. 4 (1990), pp. 401–18

Jane Dunn, *Antonia White: A Life*. London, 1998

Paul Elie, "Bartleby in the Prairie: The Unspent Life of J.F. Powers", *Harper's*, September 2013
——*The Life You Save May Be Your Own: an American Pilgrimage, New York*, 2003

Maud Howe Elliott, Uncle *Sam Ward and his Circle*. New York, 1937

Martin L. Fainsod, *James W. Wadsworth: The Gentleman from New York*. Syracuse, 1975

Daniel Fink, *Barns of the Genesee Country, 1790–1915*. Geneseo, NY, 1987

Janet Flanner, "Dearest Edith", *New Yorker*, February 22, 1929

Amos Tuck French (ed.), *Some Letters from "Chan" 1886–1926 for a Chosen Few*. Chester, NH, 1939

Mavis Gallant, *Paris Notebooks*. New York, 1988

Alden Hatch, *The Wadsworths of the Genesee*. New York, 1959

References

Lawrence Hewitt, *Port Hudson, a Confederate Bastion in the Mississippi*. Baton Rouge, 1994

Eric Homberger, *Mrs Astor's New York*. New Haven, 2002

Kathryn Hughes, "Famous People are Also Banal", *Guardian Weekly*, February 4, 2011

Ivan Illich and David Cayley, *The Rivers North of the Future: The Testament of Ivan Illich as Told to David Cayley*. Toronto, 2004

Helène Iswolsky, *No Time to Grieve: An Autobiographical Journey from Russia to Paris to New York*. Philadelphia, 1985

Kathryn Alamong Jacob, *King of the Lobby: The Life and Times of Sam Ward*. Baltimore, 2010

Norma Jacobsen, *In Recovery: The Making of Mental Health Policy*. Nashville, TN, 2004

Stephane Kirkland, *Paris Reborn: Napoleon III, Baron Haussmann and the Quest to Build a Modern City*. New York, 2013

John F. Krumwiede, *"Old Waddy's Coming": The Military Career of Brigadier James S. Wadsworth*. Baltimore, 2002

Kathleen Kutolowski, *The Social Composition of Political Leadership: Genesee County New York, 1811–1860*. New York, 1989

Hermione Lee, introduction to Antonia White, *Strangers*. London, 1980
——*Edith Wharton*. London, 2005

Andre Levity, *F. Scott Fitzgerald: A Biography*. New York, 1983

R.W.B. Lewis, *Edith Wharton: A Biography*. New York, 1975

Donna M. Lucey, *Archie and Amelie: Love and Madness in the Gilded Age*. New York, 2006

Dwight McDonald, "The Foolish Things of the World: Dorothy Day", *New Yorker*, October 4 and 11, 1952

Larissa MacFarquhar, "East Side Story", *New Yorker*, February 25, 2008

Wayne Mahood, *General Wadsworth*. New York, 2002

James R. Mellow, *Invented Lives: F. Scott Fitzgerald and Zelda*. Boston, 1982

William D. Miller, *Dorothy Day: A Biography*. New York, 1982

Elting R. Morison (ed.), *The Letters of Theodore Roosevelt*. Vol. 2. Cambridge, MA, 1951

Andrea Olmstead, *Who Was F. Scott Fitzgerald's Daisy?* Smashbooks, 2012
——*Roger Sessions. New York, 2007*

Edward Motley Pickman, *The Mind of Latin Christendom*. Oxford, 1937

Henry Pearson, *James S. Wadsworth of Geneseo*. New York, 1913

Jane Hanna Pease, *Romantic Novels, and Romantic Novelist: Francis Marion Crawford*. Bloomington, Indiana, 2011

Christopher T. Rand, *Silver Diaspora: A Journey from the Hudson Aristocracy*. Network, 2014.

Grace C. Root, *Women and Repeal*. New York, 1934

Ned Rorem, *Setting the Tone: Essays and a Diary*. New York, 1983

John Rousmaniere, *Davis Polk & Wardwell: To the Modern Era*. New York, n.d.

William Logie Russell, *The New York Hospital: A History of the Psychiatric Service, 1771–1936*. New York, 1945

Lloyd Sederer, "Moral Therapy and the Problem of Morale", *American Journal of Psychiatry*, vol. 134, no. 3 (March 1977), pp. 267–72

Richard Severo, "Where Heathcliff is Just the Boy Next Door", *New York Times*, June 10, 1975

Elizabeth Shanland, *Theatrical Feast in Paris from Molière to Deneuve*. New York, 1975

Andrew Sheehan, *Peter Maurin: Gay Believer*. New York, 1959

Elaine Showalter, *The Civil Wars of Juliet Ward Howe*. New York, 2016

Alexander Stille, "The Strange Victory of Padre Pio", *New York Review of Books*, October 25, 2012

Robert Tangman, "The Songs of Theodore Chanler", *Modern Music* 22 (May–June 1945), pp. 227–33

Louise Hall Tharp, *Three Saints and a Sinner*. Boston, 1957

Evan Thomas, *The War Lovers: Roosevelt, Lodge, Hearst and the Rise of Empire*. New York, 2010

Lately Thomas, *Sam Ward King of the Lobby*. Boston, 1965
——*A Pride of Lions. New York, 1971*
——*The Astor Orphans. Albany, 1999*

Victoria Ethier Villamil, *A Singer's Guide to American Art Song 1870–1980*. Lanham, MD, 1993, pp. 93–98

Geoffrey C. Ward, *A Disposition to Be Rich*. New York, 2012

Jennifer Weber, *Copperheads: The Rise and Fall of Lincoln's Enemies in the North*. New York, 2004

Nicholas Fox Weber, *Patron Saints: Three Rebels who Opened America up to Modern Art, 1928–1943*. New York, 1992

Edith Wharton, *A Backward Glance*. New York, 1934

Antonia White [Airene Botton], *Frost in May*. London, 1933, reprinted 1986

Claire Nicolas White, *The Death of the Orange Trees*. New York, 1963

Owen Wister, *Roosevelt: The Story of a Friendship*. New York, 1934

www.ingramcontent.com/pod-product-compliance
Lightning Source LLC
Chambersburg PA
CBHW021228090426
42740CB00006B/431